Gutsy

(Mis)Adventures in Canadian Church Planting

Jared Siebert

All proceeds from the sale of this book go to the New Leaf Network.

New Leaf Network Press, 4315 Village Centre Court, Mississauga, Ontario, CANADA

For more information contact;
info@newleafnetwork.ca
www.newleafnetwork.ca

Cover design by Lisa Howden

ISBN: 978-0-9953054-0-3

First Edition: September 2016

10 9 8 7 6 5 4 3 2 1

For all of the fearless and beautiful people who continue to plant new kinds of churches in Canada.

Contents

Foreword i

Introduction 1

Why Do This Study At All? 8

Overall Findings 18

Stay in Contact with Reality 24

Watch Your Heart 50

Be Ready for Growing Pains 59

Do You Know What Success Looks Like? 70

Know Your People 78

Always Expect the Unexpected 85

Take a LITTLE Help from Your Friends 95

Broaden Your Shoulders 103

Keep 'Em Separated 111

Your Denomination Matters 120

God Ain't Done With You Yet 133

A One-Shot Deal? 143

Conclusion 149

Acknowledgements 154

Foreword

by Joe Manafo

I will never plant a church again.

I had the best church planting experience one could ask for. I planted alongside the best people, who were also my best friends. The location was perfect, the setting ideal and the timing, just right.

However, I also lost seven prime earning years and drained my RRSPs. The emotional toll, marital strain, and relational pitfalls were considerable. The vocational pressure and confusion it carried, substantial.

Yet, I am able to look back at that season of my life and say with all honesty that it was the most meaningful adventure of which I have been a part, and the most fulfilling work I have done. For all its blemishes, it was a magical ride right from the very beginning.

In 2005, nearly a year before we planted theStory in Sarnia, Ontario, Jared Siebert took Nathan Colquhoun (one of the theStory's co-planters) and me on a road trip to visit a handful of church plants already underway. My sense was that the goal of the trip was to assure us that what we were about to do was in fact possible, and a legitimate expression of the local church.

It was on that trip, on an innocent walk in Kingston, Ontario, that it dawned on me that someone should tell the story of these churches and their planters. At that time church planting was in vogue and many "success stories" were being broadcast via blogs, books and conferences. But none of those stories were Canadian.

So, partly as a research project for our own venture, and partly from a desire to tell a Canadian story, *One Size Fits All?: Exploring New and Evolving Forms of Church in Canada* was researched, filmed and edited between 2006-2008, all the while trying to get our own church plant off the ground. Then, from 2008 until 2011, I "toured" the film hitting conferences big and small, colleges, universities, seminaries, churches, a few private showings, some radio and TV interviews, and countless one on one coffee dates all to talk about what was going on and what could be.

What Jared does in the following pages is continue this conversation and make it public. This book is not a sequel to the original film. The beauty, sorrow and wisdom contained in this report goes far beyond the experiences of 19 church planters and has no expiry date.

These reflections prevail in church planters past and present. They linger in me. Many times while reading the draft manuscript I found myself muttering under my breath things like: "I remember that" or "Didn't see that one coming" or "I really wish I had known that then". I still feel them. Most of them still haunt me. I continue to sort through some—and from others—I'm on the run.

The questions and experiences that Jared is about to unpack are not unique to me or the planters that came before me; what you're about to read has an enduring quality. You're about to discover yourself in these pages, in what has come before you, and you will inevitably, hope-fully, carry it into the future no matter where it leads.

As I write these words the church I helped plant is about to celebrate its 10ᵗʰ anniversary -without me- and it feels strange. By my own choosing, I was present for just the first seven years. Yet Jared's work here is prompting me to pay attention once again.

I feel the tug to pay attention to why I feel what I feel, to remember those who were around me then and notice those around me now, to reflect on why I pastor and lead a church when most days I feel both unfit and under qualified.

This book will ask you too, to pay attention. Not to pay attention because there's a scorecard with your name on it or because there's a secret recipe for planting a successful church but to pay attention because planting a church is more about what the Good Lord wants to do in you than what He wants to do through you.

So to the ones who were kind enough to show Jared and I how they were paying attention; to the ones whom Jesus continues to adore; to the ones who are more than the functions they perform, a few simple words for you:

To Rob Abbot: I left The Gig the day we filmed inspired. Partly by what you had managed to pull together, but mostly because I found you to be absolutely genuine. Thank you for paying attention.

To David Brazzeal: Everything you told me about Curieux gave me a new appreciation for the work that is required to gather francophone church communities. Thank you for paying attention.

To Nick Brotherwood: You're a hero in my books, beyond your work with Emerge and beyond your dedication to the Anglican Church of Canada. Your presence is a faithful one. Thank you for paying attention.

To Gary Castle: What you did, and continue to do, for Next Church is hall of fame material. I love you, friend. Thank you for paying attention.

To Kristen Cato: You struck me as a courageous woman, and what you helped shape at The Open House was fearless. Thank you for paying attention.

To Kate Dewhurst: You were so sincere the day we filmed you at The Agora, and it left me encouraged. I hope you're still contagious. Thank you for paying attention.

To Al Doseger: I cannot imagine the last ten years without your friendship and without Rustle's steadfast work. You are a gift to me and I love you dearly. Thank you for paying attention.

To Cyril Guerette: You exemplified for us through Freedomize how to lead, pastor and transition church plants into their adolescent years. Thank you for paying attention.

To Pernell Goodyear: I know we joke to extremes, but without The FRWY there is no theStory. You are a leader worth following, and I have been so happy to follow your lead. Thank you for paying attention.

To Jamie Howison: Listening to you, and to the story of St. Benedict's Table, unlocked my appreciation for a liturgical approach to church planting. Side note: the day we met you turned me on to Robert Farrar Capon and that, for me, has been a game changer. Thank you for paying attention.

To David Manafo: Under some bad advice during the editing process I cut nearly all of The Westside Gathering's story from the final version of the film. It was a mistake. I am so glad you proved me wrong. Thank you for paying attention.

To Kyle Martin: You and The Open House were the right thing, at the right place, at the right time. Well done. Thank you for paying attention.

To Paul Moores: Your approach with Living Room Church taught me to love my neighbourhood and helped me zero in on, and be faithful to, what was right before me. Thank you for paying attention.

To Joseph Moreau: I loved your love for Ecclesiax. You were, without a doubt, a gift to that community. Thank you for paying attention.

To Greg Paul: I sensed so much fight in you and in Sanctuary the day I visited. It was a good thing. Thank you for paying attention.

To Helen Ramfield: Your take on St. Benedict's Table brought perspective to me that church planting isn't just a pastor's game. Thank you for paying attention.

To Kim Reid: It was very obvious to me with The Open Door (and your other adventures) that you were doing everything God was asking you to do. Your love for people led the way. Thank you for paying attention.

To Domenic Ruso: It saddens me that we've lost touch, but I have continued to follow your movements—from The Embassy up to your present church plant—from afar. Thank you for paying attention.

To David Sawler: One of the best parts about you and your work with Lighthouse is that you operate as if you have nothing to prove and no ego to speak of. I wish I could clone you. Thank you for paying attention.

To Brad Somers: I found you to be determined to make something work where it technically shouldn't. Pax North is proof that you know what you're doing. Thank you for paying attention.

To Scott Williams: You were one of the firsts on the scene and that always comes with a price. Club 365 was a good gig. You should be so proud. Thank you for paying attention.

And thank you, Jared, for outlasting the trends and for becoming the expert in your field for the benefit of the Canadian church landscape. What you've pulled together in these pages, and in your work with the New Leaf Network, sets the stage for what's next. I can feel it. Thank you for paying attention.

That said, I will never plant a church again.

But this book just might change my mind.

Joe Manafo
Saskatoon, SK
Summer 2016

1

Introduction

How it all began...

"I think that what we tried, and what all the other experimental plants in Canada tried, is valuable."

- Kim Reid of the Open Door, Montreal

Over the past 20 years there has been a lot of pioneering church planting going on in Canada. This gutsy pioneer work has come and gone with little fanfare. In fact, if you haven't paid close attention, it could have passed you by. Sadly, if it disappears entirely in the Canadian church's rear-view mirror, I believe an important piece of our history and an opportunity for self-understanding will disappear with it. We can't let that happen.

In 2008, my good friend Joe Manafo was in the beginning stages of church planting and had a lot of unanswered questions. Why? Because Joe and his co-conspirators, Nathan Colquhoun and Darryl "The Little One" Silvestri, were trying to start something *new*. When they talked about starting something *new* they didn't just mean another church. They were after a new kind of church—and they knew they weren't alone. There were others in Canada that recognized they wanted, even needed, a new kind of church too. So Joe and his friends set off on a road trip to film a documentary and find out what these new and evolving forms of church were all about.

I was a lucky bystander in this whole project. I got to tag along for some of the filming—partly out of my own curiosity, and partly because they needed a guy who could work a soldering iron. What Joe and his friends found out there on the road was assembled into a documentary in 2008 and titled *One Size Fits All?* While it did not win an Oscar or break box office records, it did do a fantastic job of describing what was going on in Canada at the time: it framed Canadian pioneer church planting, openly wondered where Canada was headed, and presented 19 churches that were taking promising first steps toward an answer.

In the nearly eight years since it was released, a majority of the churches featured in *One Size Fits All?* have changed. In fact, only a small handful look now like they did at the time. Some no longer exist. So what happened? Did these churches represent the future or was it all a dream? If they were onto something, what can we learn from their stories? If we want to build on what they did, what do we need to know about their foundation? These questions have come up for me often in the years since 2008, especially in my own work as a denominational leader.

The book you now hold in your hands is my best attempt at some answers. Starting around 2010 or so I began bugging Joe to film a follow-up story to *One Size Fits All?* At the time, we were both vaguely aware that the story might not be a rosy one. We knew that some of the churches had closed, and that some of the planters had moved on to other things. We knew that some of the story was going to be painful. We talked it through, and concluded that there wasn't much to be gained by dredging all of that up for our friends. We also feared that if the story wasn't handled well it could even discourage future planters who were

---

¹If you haven't had the chance to see the film it's available for free online. It's well worth your time. http://onesizefitsall.ca/

dreaming of a new kind of church. Best to let sleeping dogs lie, we thought.

But the dogs kept stirring.

In 2011, Nick Brotherwood, one of the participants in the original documentary (he's the guy with the British accent representing the Montréal church plant "Emerge"), hosted a brave and honest workshop at a church planting conference that I attended. If you've ever been to a church planting conference you'll know that these are arenas where planters tend to promote all their biggest and best success stories. For some participants, like myself, the churches that get to take the stage seem to do battle with the comparatively flailing church plants we lead back home. The successful churches are huge; ours are small. Theirs are growing and easy; ours are slow, difficult, and full of tough people who lead tough lives. Those who plan church planting conferences mean well—they mean to encourage, to exemplify what is possible—but if you're not careful, you can be left feeling like a failure. After all, most church plants in Canada aren't raging successes. Most take years to establish themselves and gain a sense of stability. They are often small—though vital—parts of their neighbourhoods. They also mean the world to the people who are a part of them. But anyways, back to Nick. Nick stood out at this conference because he cut against the grain: Nick shared the story of how his church plant had closed. For me, his story had a value above and beyond a traditional success story. Why? His story sounded a lot like mine. He knew about struggle. He had survived and learned hard lessons. He was transparent about what had happened when his dreams came crashing down. Nick's story had value for me *because* it wasn't a traditional success story.

The dogs were now officially awake and weren't going to lie back down.

Now, the challenge became how to best to go about tracing the stories of the church plants from eight years previous into the present. Should it become another documentary? A series of blog posts? A podcast? I knew that whatever medium I chose I wanted the participants to be as comfortable, open, and honest as possible—not everyone in the documentary would feel as brave as Nick had at the conference.

In 2014, during my sabbatical, I decided to see if the people we had originally filmed wanted to participate in a new project. After a few initial conversations it became clear that putting people on camera again was not going to be a good idea. If I wanted people to be free to tell their whole story, I was going to need to preserve their anonymity. So, I decided to do private interviews, transcribe what was said, and then tell the story from the perspective of the group, not the individuals. At first, I thought this would result in a written report; however, I underestimated the volume of insights I received. The book that you now hold is the fruit of these conversations, in addition to many hours of processing, and a whole lot of soul-searching. I hope it proves as nourishing to you as it has to me.

Limits of Scope

A research project of this nature has the potential to lead in any number of directions. I decided to limit the scope of this project in the interest of: 1) actually completing the project, and 2) drawing out some *main* principles of these stories worth bringing into the current church planting conversation. I also recognize that I am only one person and have limits to my capacity to process information. So here are some of the limits that I placed on this project.

The first limit was on who participated. While the 19 churches featured in the original documentary were a fair cross section of what was happening in Canada at the time, they didn't represent all of what was happening. Some great churches didn't make the final cut of the film due to technical problems, timing issues, and other challenges. I recognized that sticking with the 19 churches in *One Size Fits All?* meant that some voices and stories weren't represented. Yet, in the interests of finishing this project and getting something out there for you to consider I decided to keep the study small. I further limited myself to interviewing only the main leaders of the churches. You won't find the thoughts and opinions of other leaders, board members, and congregants in this study, and I acknowledge that these contain valuable parts of the story which will remain untold for the time being.

I especially regret being unable to share the full stories of the spouses of the planters; I wasn't able to interview enough of them to be confident that I could share their story accurately. I will share what I did uncover, but more work needs to be done in this domain. In fact, to do this often-overlooked story justice would require an entirely new research project. If time permits in the future, I may return to this area for further research.

In a very small number of cases, I had to speak to people who didn't actually appear in the original film. I made this call in order to fill out some of the narratives. In some cases, people who appeared in the film did not want to participate and so I had to talk to others. In other cases, I ran out of time in contacting them.

All told, I conducted 24 interviews, so I'm confident in the story I am telling.

I'd like to take a moment here to thank all of you who did participate. You were so generous with your time and stories. You are gutsy and generous people—you're my heroes! I feel a tremendous weight of responsibility in representing your thoughts, insights, and advice. I hope you will be happy with the results.

Secondly, I'd like to affirm that this project is hopelessly time bound. The stories of these people and their churches are only half-written. So when I say I'm looking at the long-term realities of pioneer church plants in Canada, I can only tell the story up until today. I don't know what the future holds. Most of the plants featured in the documentary in 2008 had been going for a few years when we filmed them. The post-documentary interviews I conducted started in 2014 and ended in 2015. So I am able to give you, in most cases, at least 10 years in the life of a pioneer church plant—not bad. Some of the stories represent a longer time span, and others shorter.

Thirdly, I'd like to note that I have consciously limited access to the participants by taking steps to anonymize the quotes I used. What you read is what they said, except for when they made context-identifying statements. So for instance a quote which says, *"The Free Methodist Church did such and such..."* will appear in the book as, *"My denomination did such and such..."* As much as possible, I tried to represent word-for-word what was said in the interviews, but I have balanced that with the anonymity I promised the participants. Anonymity created an interview space in which participants could share openly and honestly, and in the end, I think the finished product is much closer to the truth than could have been achieved otherwise.

Methodology

It should be said from the outset that I am not a social scientist nor a professional researcher. This is also my first kick at the whole long-form writing thing. My apologies in advance, dear reader. This project is, first and foremost, a labour of love. A significant number of these stories are told by friends of mine, and I have been an active part of at least three of the churches featured. So, I make no promises of pure, scientific objectivity. That being said, as much as possible, I have tried to avail myself of the best advice and disciplines of social scientists and research practitioners. I was especially helped by the book *Discovery of Grounded Theory.*[2] I used a lot of the processes and the disciplines outlined therein to inform my practices.

---

[2] Glaser, Barney G., Anslem L. Strauss, "The Discovery of Grounded Theory: Strategies for Qualitative Research", Aldine Publishing Company, 1967.

Here is a brief overview of my research process: I used pre-determined questions for all of the interviews. These questions remained consistent throughout the project. I allowed a little "off-roading" during the interviews in order to fill out gaps in the narrative and allow for new insights. The interviews were recorded and transcribed for later reference. The next phase of the project was to re-listen to all of the interviews and pay special attention to wording and themes. I then took all those themes and began to build my theoretical framework for this book. Once the framework was built, I referred back to my notes and audio to collect exact quotes from the material. Where necessary, I contacted participants again and clarified details with them.

The final writing phase was to collect, curate, and present the information. Each chapter represents a distinct theme discovered during the interviews. Each chapter title is followed by a one-sentence distillate of the theme. This is followed by a direct quote from one of the participants that reinforces the theme. Quotes are then used throughout the chapter to clarify and deepen the basic theme and to tie us back to lived reality.

Okay, let's dig in.

2

Why Do This Study At All?

The goal of this project is to develop and deepen the practice of pioneer church planting in the Canadian context.

"I think failure is a difficult topic for the church in North America. We don't have a mechanism for dealing with failure. We don't even have a mechanism for dealing with success either. We don't usually bother asking those questions. We just write it down to a charismatic leader and that there were no underpinning principles. It doesn't seem like we're very inquisitive about how things work."

This book is about a few important things. It's about failure and success. It's about learning to ask better questions as a community about previous church planting attempts. It's about looking for underlying principles. It's about asking how we can do things better in Canada.

So what's so special about the 19 churches studied here? How can they help us do things better? The short answer is that I believe these pioneer church plants have something unique to offer the Canadian church.

First, their value to the Canadian church is in acting as pioneers. Pioneers in research, in science, in social movements, and in any other discipline make incalculable contributions to their respective communities—especially if their community is stuck or stagnated. Pioneers matter because they look for and often find a new way forward. For them, however, success is harder to come by. Success for a pioneer is two-fold: they must not only succeed in what they do, but they must also find a new way to do it. To succeed at one and fail at the other is not really success at all. To be a pioneer in the field of church planting is no exception. Success, for pioneer planters, not only means establishing a new church, but establishing a new *kind* of church.

The idea that the church in Canada is in a period of stagnation is hardly controversial—we are indeed slowly shrinking. Much of the "new growth" we see in our "successful" churches comes from Christians moving from one church to another. This includes many of our successful "fastest-growing" church plants as well. We have lost much of our capacity to invite average Canadians into the good news life we say we believe in. This is why understanding the work of pioneer church planters is so vital. Pioneer planters not only teach us what works, in terms of sharing the good news, but they teach us what is possible. They have something unique to offer in terms of pointing the way out of our current situation.

The second way pioneer planters are of value to the Canadian church is that they can teach us how to effectively engage with new categories and cultures within Canada. There is lots of pioneering work going on all over the place. There is pioneering work among new immigrant groups, among unreached people groups, and even among emerging sub-categories of established Canadian life. Pioneer stories matter, both in their successes *and* in their failures. The 19 churches featured in *One Size Fits All?* were pioneers too. They showed promise in their work among a relatively specific and often-overlooked group of Canadians, namely, the so-called "nones." Nones are a growing cultural sub-category in the Canadian mission field. They play a big role in where the future of Canada is headed. So who are these people?

"Nones" are defined by Canadian researchers as those who have no religious affiliation. The study largely responsible for naming this group is titled "Canada's Changing Religious Landscape."[3] This 2013 study, developed by the Pew Research Institute, observed changes in religious affiliation and participation among Canadians over the past 40 years. Several interesting discoveries emerged. The first was the steady decline in numbers of people identifying with both Catholic and Protestant churches in Canada, the heavier bleed coming from the Protestant camp. Next, the study noted that other religions— that is, other than Christianity—are on the rise. The breakout group in the "other religions" category is Islam. The percentage of Canadians who belong to Islam has doubled in size over the past 40 years from 2% to 4%. Why is that? Is there a Muslim equivalent of Billy Graham doing evangelism in Canada? Not exactly. A majority of the growth of Islam is *not* primarily due to conversion but to immigration. As a side note, in response to the unique missionary opportunity that a major influx of Muslims into Canada represents, the Canadian church has organized the Canadian Network for Ministry to Muslims. This is an important pioneer work which needs to be understood and celebrated. It's part of our future. Finally, the most significant finding of the study was that it revealed that the fastest growing category in Canada is the nones—people with no religious affiliation. This represents a massive cultural shift. In the past 40 years, this category has grown by 500%. Unlike the growth of Islam, this is not primarily a story of immigration. This is about mass conversion. One in four Canadians have converted from an identification with Christianity to an overtly and decidedly secular worldview over the past 40 years.

---

[3] http://www.pewforum.org/2013/06/27/canadas-changing-religious-landscape/

It could be argued that nothing material has changed for the Canadian church over the past 40 years. Forty years ago, 87% of Canadians identified as Christians; today 66% do. 66% is still a majority, so why complain? Isn't this just a problem for so-called mainline denominations? Evangelical numbers, thanks to immigration and other factors, have remained fairly steady under the circumstances. Plus, one could contend, did we ever really have the majority in the first place? Identifying as a Christian on a survey does little to confirm that you actually are one. Truly Christian people have always been the minority... If you take these narrow views of the religious landscape of Canada, it can be hard to see what all the fuss is about. But failing to see the problem doesn't really change the facts. The reality is that fewer and fewer Canadians are finding the Christian worldview compelling enough to identify with, and this is serious. People converting away from a generally Christian set of assumptions, beliefs, and values to a generally secular set of assumptions, beliefs, and values is a real problem. Canadian churches, of all stripes and denominations, need to sit up and take notice. This trend reveals the end of Christendom in Canada in stark clarity. And the end of Christendom is a real game changer for the Canadian church.

Under recent Christendom in Canada our missionary task, generally speaking, was understood as trying to convince Canadians to make real what they already said they believed. Since Canadians were already Christianesque, almost by default, we had a lot of raw material to work with: religious memory, generalized goodwill, and a vague sense that we were the good guys and could be counted on to lead society in a healthy direction. This is no longer the case. The fact that a growing number of Canadians now belong to and identify with another belief system entirely changes how the church needs to operate in Canada. It's hardly controversial to make this claim. What may be controversial, however, is to suggest any course of action other than mourning the loss of our highly-favoured position in society. Yet, complaining won't change things—it will only cement the divide. At this stage in the trend, many of the nones may still be nominally or culturally secular, just as they were nominally or culturally Christian. But as the trend continues, their position will become more and more entrenched.

The rise of secularism has created new missionary challenges for the church. For starters, there is a greater cultural distance between the church and average Canadians than there ever has been before. If we want to meaningfully engage with what is, for all intents and purposes, a new people group in our country, we have to be willing to do some hard work. Waiting for them to come around to our way of seeing things isn't an option. Missionaries, when faced with a cultural divide, have to do the hard work of understanding. They find ways to uncover plausibility structures, language, meaning-making, and basic perceptions of the Jesus story. They spend time learning the intricacies of the local language so that they can communicate the story in a way that is understood. They act as translators and as bridge-builders. They don't wait for culture to come to them— they go to the culture. They work on its terms, with its categories, and on its timetable. In Canada this kind of work is still in its infancy.

So what does this have to do with the 19 churches in the documentary? Well, these churches were—by and large— engaging with people who were on their way out or had already left the church—the nones—just before they became nones. This is why these planters believed so deeply in what they were doing. This was an act of love for them. They recognized what they were doing as the beginning of an important missionary work in Canada. They stood as pioneers on the fringes of a new Canadian frontier. So, when their church plants struggled or closed, the consequences felt all the more desperate. This was missionary work ending before it really got started. If they had played it safe and operated a little farther from Christendom's borderlands, the risks wouldn't have been as high—most of their members would have found another church to belong to. But that's not how pioneer church planting works among the nones. Pioneer church plants often operate as the last stop on the train ride out of Christianity. The true value of these 19 churches is what they learned doing ministry in this context. They may not have had it all figured out but they do now know what it takes to hang in there with the nones. As this trend continues to work its way through our country, we'll need to understand their stories more and more. In these pioneer churches are the seeds of our future.

A third value in these pioneer planting stories is that these stories are Canadian. Now, I'm not for a second suggesting that stories from pioneers in other countries have nothing to teach us. They most certainly do. It's just that these particular stories, precisely because they are Canadian, have special value for us.

I want to go on record as saying that Canadian Christians demonstrate a dangerous apathy toward our own stories. I first saw this when I got involved in planning conferences. Canadians are not generally drawn to conferences that feature Canadian speakers and stories. We say that we are, but we aren't. We prove this over and over with our actions. If you want Canadians to come and hear Canadians, you need to first fill the stage with speakers and stories from the U.S. and then sneak Canadians onto the platform when no one is looking. Sure, you'll get demolished on the comment cards for lack of Canadian content, but at least you'll have actually hosted a conference that people attended. Why is this? I'm not sure. But I see it, consistently. It's not just limited to the church either. It's in the air. Canadian television, Canadian movies, Canadian music, Canadian art, and Canadian companies all have an uphill battle if they want to be heard above their counterparts south of the border. This isn't xenophobia. It's just life in the Great White North, and it's as much a part of our identity as maple syrup and hockey.

One last observation before I conclude this point. I find it interesting that there is already a formal network for Ministry to Muslims in Canada. This is a positive move for the Canadian church. Muslim immigration represents an unprecedented missionary opportunity for deep friendship, for pointing the way to global peace, and for new people groups to give their lives to Jesus. The Canadian church stands to be a far richer place. But why has it taken us so long to also start a network for ministry to the nones? I think it's blindness. Both groups represent part of the Canadian future and yet we only have a network for one?

To reiterate, a key value of these 19 stories is that they are from a Canadian context. One participant put it like this: *"You don't need to go across the pond to find a mission. As lush and easy as it is here, we still have gaping holes in our souls."* These Canadian stories remind us of the mountain of work we have to do right here in our own country. Another participant I interviewed said, *"One of my big frustrations with the church is that people don't seem to feel any sense of urgency about the work we do."* I think that if we allow them to, these stories will help restore a sense of urgency. We have a lot of work to do among the people of Canada—work we had better be doing.

A fourth value of pioneer church plants in our Canadian context is that there is simple value in inquiry. People are curious about the things they care about. Inquiry is a way to get serious about the work that God has given us to do. Here's what one of the participants had to say about the importance of pioneer planting:

"Our unwillingness to inquire is a serious concern for me. There is a generation of possible, would-be church planters, who are now about 15 or 16, and they are watching from the wings. They are watching what happens to these poor suckers who are saying to themselves and others, 'You know, I think God might be asking us to try something new here.' You know, they're smart cookies. They're watching and seeing what happens—especially if something doesn't turn out so well. And they'll be making decisions based on that. So it's not responsible to not inquire about what happened [with these pioneer plants]."

Many of the participants agreed to participate because they wanted to be an encouragement to others, especially other planters who want to plant at the edges of Canadian Christendom. Those whose church plants closed were very worried that their stories might deter people from trying. One said, *"I think it should be done again. I will not discourage anyone from trying this."* I hope that this project honours those intentions.

On a final note, the value of pioneer planters is also in the ability for their contributions to live on through a larger community. This is an important process. It depends not only on the brave work of pioneers but also on the capacity of a larger community to listen, to learn, and to build on what has gone before them. Without a connection to a larger community, the work of pioneers does little to change things in any permanent way. That was also the primary work of this book: first to listen and then to learn. The next task for a pioneer is to offer the results of such learning and listening to a larger community. It is then up to the larger community to use this material in future efforts.

So, dear reader, this means that we will need to do some heavy lifting together. I have started the sorting process but you are going to have to take this the rest of the way. As we go, let's keep a few things in mind.

The first is to be open-minded and critical of what you read. As one participant put it,

"Many people don't see young leaders or fringe thinkers as having any insight because they are not old enough or experienced enough—which is the category of wisdom. So I think we can gain some insight by listening to young leaders and new leaders. Although we may not be ready to put it in our wisdom bucket—as in say it's all right—[these leaders] are insightful enough to pay attention to."

As I mentioned earlier, I've started the sorting process. I didn't consider everything I heard in the interviews as strong insight. I didn't think that some of it should even be considered as good advice. Moreover, not everything I present to you in this book should be considered wisdom. Time and testing are required to convert learning into wisdom.

The second thing you'll need to keep in mind is that these are real people's stories. It's easy to see a play developing in a hockey game when you're watching it on TV. It's another thing altogether when you're wearing the skates and holding the stick. Resist the temptation of armchair coaching and second-guessing. Let the planter tell the story their way. Joe strove for accuracy in his film. I tried to do the same. One planter saw the documentary this way:

> *"I think that Joe managed to tell our story pretty accurately and pretty positively. I also think the follow-up story is really important. The film also carries for me, some pain. Not just because of how my own story turned out in the end, but moreso because of how things turned out for some of my other friends who were also featured in the film."*

These stories are deeply personal. These church planters are real people who stepped out and did something new. They put it all on the line and they deserve respect for that. They were pioneers—the first to try and do what they tried to do, where they tried to do it. That takes guts. At the time, they didn't have the support of an entire shelf in the Christian bookstore lending credibility to what they were attempting, and some of them paid a high price for that. We owe them respect, and we need to let their stories speak for themselves and avoid rushing to judgement.

The third thing to keep in mind is to guard yourself against pessimism. The pioneer's penalty exists but so does the pioneer's reward. Many of the participants spoke enthusiastically about what they got to do and see. For example,

"There is a stronger sense of joy and of accomplishment. The people I got to meet, work with, wrestle with, fight with, and disagree with. I never would have gotten that experience if I hadn't stepped out."

There are unexpected benefits to doing something new. There are possibilities and experiences that are simply not available to those that stick to the well-travelled roads deep inside Christendom. One participant bragged, *"I can think of no other thing I would rather have done. I think I have the best job in the Canadian church."* So, if you feel called to pioneer church planting, take heart. There are plenty of great reasons to step out and do what you are about to do.

Finally, one planter had this advice: *"Think for yourself more—don't just copy models."* As you read these pages you may tempted to uncritically copy something you read. The goal of the larger community should not be to reproduce what has happened before, but to build on it. If you are about to plant, remember that these stories belong to someone else, and your story belongs to you. Their stories offer something to consider and learn from, but they aren't meant to be repeated. If we are to progress, we are going to have to commit ourselves to building on what has gone on before.

3

Overall Findings

There were at least 12 factors that contributed, either negatively or positively, to the overall health of pioneer church plants.

> *"A lot of my co-workers didn't pioneer a new way of being the church. They didn't climb as high in the tree to look for hard-to-reach fruit. They didn't join us up there, and instead seemed to be content with their lives where they were at. Those that did climb higher paid a price for it. Some of that is the muck I created myself. Some of it just comes with the territory."*

The central question of this study is what—of the muck—is self-created and what just comes with the territory? That is a tough question to tease out and to do it well we'll need to go step by step. The first step is making sense of the overall survival numbers: how many of the 19 fledgling churches in our sample survived and how many didn't. The overall number will allow us to define the pioneer's penalty for our 19 churches.

Here is what I found: when I re-visited the churches in 2014 and 2015, I discovered that 52% of the 19 churches were continuing their work in more or less the same manner as they had in the film—they survived. For the remainder of this book we'll frequently refer to these churches as "continuing churches." The other 48% were no longer continuing in the manner in which we filmed them—they didn't survive. For the remainder of this book we'll frequently refer to these church plants as "non-continuing" churches.

The choice to define these 19 churches using terms like "continuing" and "non-continuing" was not a simple decision. Terms like "continuing" and "non-continuing" are a little imprecise. Traditional terms like "success" or "failure" are more precise. While more precise, they still don't seem to apply very well to what actually happened. Here's what I mean: in 20% of the non-continuing cases, the church plants stopped functioning and one or even two new churches immediately formed out of the ashes. While it's hard to call that a complete failure, it's hard to call it a success either. The fact that a church had closed was a source of grief to everyone involved. The planter and the team had not meant for this to happen. Sure, it turned out all right in the end, but that was more Providence than a plan. In the remaining 80% of the non-continuing cases, things were a little simpler. Once these church plants stopped functioning, the congregants moved on to join other churches, began a churchless faith, or sadly now have no faith at all.

Another question for us to consider is what a 52% survival rate actually means. Is that a good number or a bad number? Well, if your business is starting restaurants then the answer is that it's good! For a restaurateur, a 52% survival rate is a great number. New restaurants only have a 40% survival rate in just the first 3-5 years.[4] Our study took place over many more years than that. But church plants aren't new restaurants. So, what if we compared our numbers against general Canadian church planting averages? Well, we can't—those statistics have yet to be established through a formal study. However, rest assured, dear reader, good research on church planting in Canada is

[4] H.G. Parsa, John T. Self, David Njite, and Tiffany King, "Why Restaurants Fail," *Cornell Hospitality Quarterly* 46 (2005), 309-312, accessed July 28, 2016, doi:10.1177/0010880405275598.

starting to emerge.[5] For now, we'll have to settle for my less-than-scientific anecdotal standards. From an informal poll of denominational leaders, I can tell you that the general Canadian church plant survival rate is around 65-75% after 10 years. The only other number I've heard tossed around is that around 2/3 of all church plants fail within the first 5 years—however, I have yet to find the study that supports this unconfirmed urban legend. So, if we follow my informal poll, of the 19 churches that I studied, 3 to 4 more churches closed than the national average. Three to four churches is the pioneer's penalty for our sample.

Another key question for our study would be: is that price too high? I guess that remains to be seen. Given the growing missionary crisis in Canada, we may soon find that the risks of *not trying* something new far outweigh the risks of *trying* something new.

I don't want to be cavalier about this. Given the very high emotional and spiritual stakes of church planting, there is something very menacing about having a 50/50 shot at surviving past your 10th year anniversary. It's even more menacing when you realize that the risks aren't just limited to the planter either. Church planting failures cost planter families and other members of the church as well. While some in this group simply moved on to another faith community, not every story turns out that way. Here's one way it can go down if your plant closes:

"When we closed some people left the church altogether. I can think of two or three couples that have walked away from their faith completely. At least two of them are self-proclaimed atheists at this time."

This can feel like a huge price to pay, especially after pouring years of your life into a group of people and a neighbourhood. The stakes are indeed high. To compound things further, the loss

---

[5] The *2015 Canadian Church Planting Survey* by Lifeway Research is an excellent example of what we can learn through broad-based research.

of a pioneering work is not only a local loss but a loss to the Canadian church at large.

One of the greatest worries that participants had in being a part of this project was that they would inadvertently dissuade future planters from taking the risk. I share their concern. Church planting is so critical a task, with so few willing to even consider it, that to thoughtlessly discourage people is reckless to say the least. That being said, I hope that in reading these stories, you discover the gritty and powerful truth that some risks are worth taking. The Canadian church's supply of cheap and quick solutions is running dry. In their absence, what will we have left beyond the costly pioneer penalties we see above? Somewhere, somehow, someone has to stand up and pick up the tab for seeing the gospel flourish in all corners of our culture.

So, what else can we draw from these survival numbers? Up until now our conclusions have been a little dark. On the bright side, these numbers mean that we now have ten important examples of churches with something to teach us about longevity in pioneering. One participant observed:

"There are actually a bunch of experienced planters now that have something to offer. We didn't have that when I started."

As for the other nine, we now have churches that know where the shoals in Canadian waters are hidden. One participant put it this way:

"You know what? We failed. In the end you could look at it and say, 'You lasted 6 years—so it didn't work.' At least we tried. We did the grand experiment and some good things— some really good things—came out of it."

If we as the Church in Canada do our work well, these "good things" don't have to stay local. If we listen well and understand well, we can draw out insights that will help future generations of pioneer church planters. Successes and failures both, in the right hands, can be precious gifts.

Themes

Apart from the overall meaning of the survival numbers themselves, the interviews provided a rich source of learning. What follows here is a quick overview of themes I gleaned over the course of the interviews. I believe they will serve pioneer planters and their churches well in the future. You can use this section as quick reference guide, and the following chapters cover each of them in greater detail.

1 - Stay in Contact with Reality

Planters who had a reality-based relationship to their dreams and aspirations did better than those who remained doggedly committed to idealism and fantasy.

2 - Watch Your Heart

Planters who watched their hearts did much better over the long run than those who left their character issues unaddressed.

3 - Be Ready for Growing Pains

Planters who unapologetically pursued becoming a healthy church did better than planters who were motivated negatively to not become a traditional church.

4 - Do You Know What Success Looks Like?

Plants that developed ways of building on success and adapting after failure did better than those that refused to examine themselves according to any standards—even their own.

5 - Know Your People

Planters and plants that were prepared to adapt to the people who actually joined them did better than those that couldn't adjust or who longed to work with people who weren't joining them.

6 - Always Expect the Unexpected
Planters and plants that persevered through unexpected events did better than those that were unable or unwilling to keep going.

7 - Take a LITTLE Help From Your Friends
Plants that received occasional or modest help from outside sources did better than those that depended heavily on outside sources for survival.

8 - Broaden Your Shoulders
Planters who were able to share leadership did better than plants in which the majority of energy and authority was localized in the planter.

9 - Keep 'Em Separated
Plants that did not tie their survival to a business did better than those that did tie their plant to a business.

10 - Your Denomination Matters
Planters who were connected with denominations with a high capacity for nurturing and supporting pioneer church planting did better than those whose denominations had little to no capacity for support and nurturing them.

11 - God Ain't Done With You Yet
Planters can and do recover when a church plant doesn't continue.

12 - A One-Shot Deal?
The future of pioneer church planting in Canada depends on planters who can overcome their reluctance to plant more than once.

4

Stay in Contact with Reality

Planters who had a reality-based relationship to their dreams and aspirations did better than those who remained doggedly committed to idealism and fantasy.

> *"We did a great job of communicating this vision of how we were going to engage missionally with the neighbourhood. But after two years you realize you're not going to save the neighbourhood. That's Jesus' job. Your job is to influence the neighbourhood through gospel life together and that means long haul-type stuff. I think some of our people were disillusioned by that."*

Nothing erodes longevity in pioneer church planting quite like disillusionment. Disillusionment can enter a church plant through the planter, through the people in the church, or both. Church plants, once infected by this disease almost always die.

Disillusionment is generated and perpetuated through a fantasy cycle. "Fantasy cycle" is a term I borrowed from the work of Christopher Booker. More on that later. For now we'll leave it at this: Church plants can be a haven for people who fantasize about belonging to a perfect church. The cycle begins when they move from church to church fleeing disillusionment and hoping to find the perfect church community. Successful, long haul pioneer church planters can break this cycle—not by offering people a perfect church—but by helping people reconnect with the reality of life together in a fallen world.

Fantasy and fantasy cycles are nothing new for the church; they are a natural part of living life with others. Dietrich Bonhoeffer described this well in his famous book, *Life Together:*

"On innumerable occasions a whole Christian community has been shattered because it has lived on the basis of a wishful image. Certainly serious Christians who are put in a community for the first time will often bring with them a very definite image of what Christian communal life [Zusammenleben] should be, and they will be anxious to realize it. But God's grace quickly frustrates all such dreams. A great disillusionment with others, with Christians in general, and, if we are fortunate, with ourselves, is bound to overwhelm us as surely as God desires to lead us to an understanding of genuine Christian community... God hates this wishful dreaming because it makes the dreamer proud and pretentious. Those who dream of this idealized community demand that it be fulfilled by God, by others, and by themselves... When their idealized image is shattered, they see the community breaking into pieces. So they first become accusers of other Christians in the community, then accusers of God, and finally the desperate accusers of themselves."[6]

Fantasy is not something churches can avoid, but something they must lead through. This goes double for pioneer church plants

---

[6] Dietrich Bonhoeffer, *Life Together and Prayerbook of the Bible,* (Minneapolis: Augsburg Fortress,1996), 35-36. Many thanks to my friend Jay Dyrland for pointing this out to me in the early stages of my writing! You're the best.

as they are especially rich soil for fantasy. Why? Because pioneer church plants desperately long for the church to be different. This is both their greatest strength and their most dire weakness. If pioneer church plants want to go the distance, they must balance their desire to be different with a strong connection to reality.

Fantasy cycles aren't limited to the church, but occur naturally wherever people are present. The book *The Neophiliacs*[7] by Christopher Booker offers a thorough description of the mechanics of the fantasy cycle process through tracing a cultural revolution in Britain in the 1950s and 60s. He lays out the fantasy cycle in five distinct stages: the Anticipation Stage, the Dream Stage, the Frustration Stage, the Nightmare Stage, and the Death Wish Stage.[8] I stumbled across the book and concept through Kester Brewin's 2006 blog post "Neophilia 3: Christian Fantasy Cycles and Stages of Faith."[9] Brewin's blog post accurately predicted that the label "emerging church" was about to die because it had gone through at least three of the five stages. As I conducted my research I found that these five stages were also useful in describing the long-term realities of pioneer church planting. In short, I found that pioneer church plants that continued found a way to break the fantasy cycle at the Frustration Stage; plants that weren't able to break the cycle eventually closed. Let's take a closer look.

The Anticipation Stage

During the Anticipation Stage "the powers that be" are responsible for widespread stagnation. That stagnation becomes the negative focus of a revolutionary group, who form around a common critique and sense of disillusionment with the status

---

[8] Christopher Booker, *The Neophiliacs: The Revolution in English Life in the Fifties and Sixties*, (London: Pimlico, 1992).

[9] Kester Brewin, "Neophilia 3: Christian Fantasy Cycles and Stages of Faith," http://www.kesterbrewin.com/2006/01/11/neophilia-3-christian-fantasy-cycles-and-stages-of-faith/, (January 11, 2006).

quo. Together they anticipate the beginning of a new world. They begin searching for "a dream-focus, a cause, a release."[10]

Let's let this play out in our context: many have recognized that the church in Canada is in trouble. It seems stagnant and stuck, and as people recognize the symptoms, they begin to worry. In response, a group of revolutionaries within the church forms to engage in what's-wrong-with-the-church conversations. And it doesn't stop there—they begin to organize what's-wrong-with-the-church conferences so that they don't feel crazily alone in their opinions, and to fill bookshelves with what's-wrong-with-the-church books. All of it is true. All of it is important. We can even say that all of it is *required* if the church is going to break out of its stagnation. Once the deconstruction project is well underway, yet another group forms to create local experiments to explore new possibilities: these are the pioneer planters. They push the conversation past what's-wrong-with-the-church and get people started on trying something new. This is what I believe I saw in the 19 churches examined in this project.

At first, for these pioneers, the most plentiful materials on the metaphorical deconstruction site are the negative visions collected during the what's-wrong-with-the-church period. For some planters, these materials act as a stopgap until they find something sturdier to build with. Unfortunately, in other plants, these materials form key parts of the foundation and frame of what is built.

As the Anticipation Stage ends, the full-scale construction project of the Dream Stage begins. Darkness gives way to light. There is a sense excitement, a burst of creative energy, and a sense of relief.

---

[10] Booker, 71

The Dream Stage

Current phase

During the Dream Stage, the revolutionaries are caught up in a collective "day-dream"[11] in which it seems as though *all* of their hopes and aspirations are about to be realized. Things seem to come together and happen all by themselves. Energy, possibilities, and ideas appear limitless.

One of the most rewarding aspects of pioneer church planting is the Dream Stage. You've talked long enough and now you're actually going to act. There is a collective sense of relief, even if you're uncertain about what the results will be. The feeling is electric—you feel alive, like you're finally operating at your full capacity as a human being. And the truth is that you are: things that happen during the Dream Stage are life-changing, and faith-building. They make you leap out of bed each day because you can't wait to see what God will do next. It can feel as though the second chapter of Acts just appeared right in the middle of your life:

> "They devoted themselves to the apostles' teaching and to fellowship, to the breaking of bread and to prayer. Everyone was filled with awe at the many wonders and signs performed by the apostles. All the believers were together and had everything in common. They sold property and possessions to give to anyone who had need. Every day they continued to meet together in the temple courts. They broke bread in their homes and ate together with glad and sincere hearts, praising God and enjoying the favor of all the people. And the Lord added to their number daily those who were being saved" (Acts 2:42-47).

This passage describes the Dream Stage for the early church. Yet, we know from reading the rest of the book of Acts that this period did not last forever but gave way to all-too-familiar human reality. The *all* and *everyone* giddiness of those early days slipped into something a little less... all-encompassing. The story of Ananias

---

[11] Booker, 71

and Sapphira ended the "everyone holding all that they had in common" streak. As more time passed, Greek widows began to wonder if their ethnicity played a factor in whether or not their needs would be met by the church. Move a little farther along in the book and the church of Acts 2 gave way to the churches of Corinth, Galatians, Smyrna, and Laodicea. The Dream Stage doesn't last forever—it never has, and it never will.

Now before we get too far ahead of ourselves, let's bask a little longer in the glow of those famous six verses of Acts 2:42-47. These six verses describe a time so good that people throughout church history have looked to them to fuel their imagination about what the church could look like in their present circumstances. The days described in these six verses are so good, so deep, and so meaningful that 2000 years later, most of us would still love a piece of that action—right here, right now.

When the pioneer planters in our study began their work, they were shooting for something that resembled those six verses. And why shouldn't they have been? A church like that would stand out like a sore thumb in any culture on earth, at any time in history. Human beings, when left to their own devices, don't naturally live this way. Everything about those six verses claims that "business as usual" has ended and a new order of things has begun. It announces that the kingdom of God has come near. It insists that God's will is being done on earth as it is in heaven. It is irrefutable evidence, even to outsiders, that God is at work in the world.

Each planter had positive things to say about their walk through the Dream Stage. For some, there was a real sense of possibility:

"Lots of what we did at that stage was 'That's great! Let's do it!' So the sky was the limit."

For others, it really was like a dream come to life:

"I was living my dream. You know how we all seem to have this thing inside of us where we want to be right in the moment—where we can express who we are, and other people see it and value it? We want to have this thing inside of us really change the world, make it a better place."

This wasn't an uncommon experience! These were life-changing, hope-creating, and faith-building moments. They were some of the best days of their lives.

So if the Dream Stage is so good and so common, then when does it become a problem? When does dreaming go wrong? The reality is that for some of the 19 churches the Dream Stage wasn't a problem at all, but for others it was. The deciding factor turned out to be the choices each church plant made when the Dream Stage ended. Plants that were able to balance reality with their dreams did better than those that didn't.

According to my observations, plants that didn't survive made an either/or choice between their dreams and their reality. Those that chose dreams at the expense of reality saw their church became trapped in the cycle. Those that chose reality at the expense of their dreams found their church stuck in despair. No planter ever winds up with the exact kind of church they imagined at the beginning. As my friend Joe Manafo likes to put it:

"First, you grab a packet of seeds labelled 'Church Plant.' Next, you plant it in the soil of your community. Then you wait. Finally, you try to love and lead whatever grows."

Yet, no planter ever winds up with a church that utterly fails to realize *any* of their dreams. It's always a mixed bag with church planting: it never is just one thing or the other. It's never just darkness or light; never just failure or success. To survive as a planter, you have to be okay with *some* of what you hoped for growing alongside *some* of what you never expected alongside of *some* of what you never wanted.

So, how can pioneer church plants navigate all of this? How should they handle their collective hopes and dreams? The advice of several participants was to think more clearly about expectations. If you're planning on starting a pioneer church, here are few questions to get the expectations conversation started with the members of your plant:

- What steps are we going to take, as a group, to ensure that we are being realistic with our expectations?

- Is there anything we are afraid to hope for because of past disappointments?

- How will we bring our collective expectations to the surface?

- What about time frames of these expectations?

- How quickly do we imagine things will unfold?

- What sorts of things do we expect to see right away?

- What sorts of things would we love to see but aren't expecting to see right away?

- Can we imagine a list of things that we know will take longer than we might want them to?

- Does our list include things like character development and discipleship as these are not overnight processes?

- Are we committed, as a group, to seeing the kinds of good that can only come from years of working through deep disappointments or hurts?

- Are we prepared for the reality that some of the things we hope for, even if they are good and right, may never come?

- Does that include the kinds of things that the church has been waiting 2000 years to see?

- Are we ready to endure together through "groaning as in the pains of childbirth" (Romans 8:22)?

- Are we ready to wait together for God to finish His work with the restoration of all things?

The hardest thing about the Dream Stage is that it doesn't last forever—just as morning mist doesn't last very long into the day. As reality sets in, unmet expectations can be really challenging for a church plant. And unmet expectations that remain unspoken and unaddressed are potentially toxic. Enter the Frustration Stage.

The Frustration Stage

This new world isn't quite what everyone dreamed it would be. Not all of the revolutionary group's dreams and expectations are plausible or even desirable. For some, the revolution has gone too far—for others, it hasn't nearly gone far enough. Tensions within the group begin to fester but still, "the drive to climax continues."[12]

The Frustration Stage can be, well, frustrating. For the first time since the start of your church plant there are tensions. And for the first time those tensions aren't predominantly coming from outside the group, but within. Personalities that once meshed so well begin to grind. Disappointment and disillusionment start to seep in. Much of the frustration flows from the idea that this church was *supposed* to be different. The Frustration Stage kicks church plants right in their identity.

Let's take the example of a church striving to be creative. Churches that pride themselves on being creative find it hard to be creative all the time. It's hard work to make every gathering an

---

[12] Booker, 71

artistic revolution—and downright impossible to meet that expectation week after week for two or three years straight. The truth is that sometimes being together needs to be a little bit boring. Sometimes, doing the same thing twice in a row is a wise use of energy. And sometimes, doing the same thing over and over again is actually conducive to forming people. This is, after all, the genius of the liturgical tradition. For the rest of the church some level of repetition is normal—expected, even. But for a church where creativity is a source of pride and identity repetition can feel downright demoralizing.

Let's try another example: churches that pride themselves on being all about relationship. These churches can struggle when, in the natural course of things, there is interpersonal conflict among members. If this is an identity piece for the church, a sense of betrayal can be highly threatening. I thought this church was supposed to different?!

In the Frustration Stage, the more deeply the planter or members of the plant are committed to their ideals the more deeply frustrated they will feel when reality doesn't appear to be forthcoming. Indeed, as we've already mentioned, plants and planters that have a reality-based relationship to their dreams and expectations do better than those that remained doggedly committed to idealism and fantasy.

So how did the plants in our study do at this stage? All of them experienced frustration. The depth of the frustration varied according to the depth at which they identified with their aspirations. Those that found a way to absorb and learn from the blows that reality dealt to their identity did better than those that doggedly resisted reality. This stage wasn't easy for anyone.

In one particular case, this stage arrived at the three year mark:

"We hit a couple of walls about three years in. We realized that we were not really doing what we said we wanted to be doing. We had to regroup."

This regrouping process took this church through a brush with burnout. They called a meeting and decided to cancel their weekly gathering for several months. They declared a Sabbath. Instead of public gatherings, they met in homes. They held regular meetings to begin re-imagining their collective identity moving forward. They wrote down what came from these conversations. This helped them clarify their collective expectations and gain a new sense of purpose. The cancelling of their gathering was such a success that they decided to make it an annual thing. Sabbath went from biblical concept to an annual community practice.

Despite all of the good that came out of this brush with burnout, it was still a deep challenge for them as a community. They considered themselves a highly relational church. The idea of engaging in formal and structured processes felt antithetical to who they were (when you have genuine relationships you don't need structures right? Right?). In the end their process of self-reflection led them to realize that if they wanted to continue being a healthy, relational church, they needed to invest in structures that would enable them to relate more deeply. They adjusted their identity from a relational church that never organized to a relational church that occasionally focused on organization. It somehow felt "less cool," but at least it maintained contact with reality.

Another plant took great pride in their no-nonsense approach to communal truth-telling with one another. This was a radical shift to the community's previous church experiences. The planter had gathered a group of revolutionaries who said that they really wanted to go deep with one another and they had set out to be unapologetically involved in one another's lives. They wanted to speak the truth to one another. Said the planter:

"You can't hide here. And that's the beauty of church plants—people say they love it because they can't hide. And we feel like we're all together and like we know each other. But when you start unfolding some of the sin and the 'why' of what we are doing as a church, some people will only allow you to go so far with them. For us those have definitely been some of the hardest moments."

That some people said that truth-telling is what they wanted and then demonstrated the opposite with their lives was extremely painful for this church plant. It was especially painful because some people chose to leave the plant after feeling that others had ganged up on them. This caused some soul-searching for the planter and the congregation. They began to work through their frustration in a positive and healthy way. They talked about how to give and receive criticism in a healthy way. They wrestled with the fact that while some people were "all in" for the truth-telling, others weren't as comfortable with it. During this time, the planter had to do a "gut check" on his disappointment that this wasn't the church he had signed up to plant. He had to balance his hopes and dreams with the reality of where people in his church were actually at. What enabled this church to survive this and other bumps along the way was that they consistently chose a reality-based relationship to their hopes and aspirations instead of a dogged commitment to idealism and fantasy; they neither abandoned their aspirations nor died to them.

As I'm sure you can imagine, not all church plants can successfully navigate the turbulent waters of the Frustration Stage. The demand that reality makes on our fantasies is often incredibly high. Sometimes it's a price communities are not willing to pay. Those who are unwilling or unable to effectively balance their expectations with reality move on to the Nightmare Stage.

The Nightmare Stage

This stage is "the reverse of the Dream Stage, in which everything goes increasingly and unaccountably wrong."[13] Energy, possibilities, and ideas are now in short supply. The project that once gave more energy than it demanded seems to be taking more than it gives. The Nightmare Stage can feel exhausting and hopeless.

People often leave a church plant at this stage, and people leaving seems to confirm that this church is not what it claimed to be to those that remain. Disillusionment sets in. People begin to believe that this church is just the same as all the others. Worse still, other churches seem to have more integrity— at least they aren't claiming to be different. Here's how one planter described this stage:

"People started to vote with their feet. And so I said, 'Wow, we really are a church after all!'"

In the Nightmare Stage, expectations are no longer being met. As each person leaves, the hope that expectations can ever be met seems to leave with them.

The stress of keeping the church going and the weight of unmet expectations can be truly debilitating for the planter. It was not uncommon for planters at this stage to take stress leaves from their plants. Unfortunately, the stress leave would often deplete the plant further, and when the planter returned the situation was even worse. Said one such planter:

"I wasn't seeing anybody really into it, and I don't know that I was as into it anymore either. So I took a sabbatical for six months. When I came back I thought I had a little bit of energy, but then six months later, we decided to end."

---

[13] Booker, 72

Disillusionment can become contagious and gain momentum. Here is how another planter described the Nightmare Stage:

"As a couple, we began to see the church as a burden. And then we'd kind of look around the room and wonder and say, 'Are we really a church?'"

Planters often felt like they were the ones left holding the bag. Most weren't able to hold out for very long.

Others remain dogged in their determination to resist reality. *"When you start to see the writing on the wall, there are just so many layers of self-denial and self-deception,"* said one planter. Some hoped to force reality into compliance by simply working harder. Others fell prey to anger and resentment: they lashed out at God, other people in the plant, and even other churches. In the end, it can often seem impossible to keep going if your efforts are not producing what you expected to see. The weight just gets heavier and heavier:

"I don't want to say that it was a mistake. A lot of people benefited from what we were doing. I watched people grow in their faith. It was well focused at the beginning. But somewhere along the way it just became heavier and heavier. It became like work."

Plants that go too deep into the Nightmare Stage rarely survive. The time to address the dissonance between expectations and reality is earlier, during the Frustration Stage. More often than not, by the time your plant feels like a nightmare, it's too late. Remarkably, some plants did manage to come back from this stage but the loss of people and momentum meant walking with a limp—often for years.

The Death Wish Stage

At the Death Wish Stage, all hope has been lost. Stagnation has set in. There is no energy to continue. For those people still committed to ignoring reality, this is simply the beginning of a new Anticipation Stage. The only difference now is that "the powers that be" are the leaders of the church plant. After all, if you remain committed to following fantasy all that is left to do is to find a new group of revolutionaries who have a "real" vision for what the church should be...

Most church plants seem to die with a whimper and not with a bang. The Death Wish Stage, as violent as that label may sound, is more often experienced as a quiet decision rather than a violent and explosive fight to the end. In the vast majority of the cases in our study, the group simply admitted that the idea had run its course and they all decided to move on. Here's how one planter described it:

"It just kind of fizzled out. We kind of canceled some events here and canceled some over there and then we just never did it again. But I still saw my people all the time. We never really closed it, it just kind of fizzled out."

While the reasons for closing were not entirely identical among the non-continuing plants, the sense that things just "fizzled out" was by far the most common experience. For most in this stage, the idea of continuing seemed more difficult than quietly deciding to close.

Only a small number of the non-continuing church plants ended in a contentious way, and "contentious" might even be too strong of a word. In most cases, closing was a relatively peaceful affair. In the "contentious" cases it was the denomination and not the plant who decided to pull the plug. Interestingly, when denominations stepped in to end a plant, often a small group of people would form a new church under a new name, and continue on without denominational support. Many of the churches that were birthed from this process continue on today.

Another interesting fact is that most non-continuing church plants in our study closed with more people and assets than they started with, meaning they closed with money in the bank, members, and often with a public space. It's odd that these assets (money, people, and property)–things that planters would give their left arm for in the early days of planting–are not enough to sustain plants in their latter days. This begs the question, what is missing in a church plant at the end of its life that seems to be there in the beginning? To me the only thing I can ascertain is that they no longer have hope. They no longer believe that what they collectively put their hands to will produce something good. Hope, in my experience, is the true fuel of a pioneer church plant. Without it bucks, buildings, and butts are meaningless. Here's how one participant put it:

> *"I still believe that one of the reasons our plant died is that some of the people–although they initially bought into the idea that we were family–didn't really believe it."*

The non-continuing plants in our study lacked the hope that they were still in it together. They lacked the hope that they all *still believed* the same things. They lacked the hope that they all still wanted to build a life together. Without collective hope, a plant cannot survive–even when they have plenty of assets.

As you can see, the fantasy cycle isn't limited to the early church or the church of Bonhoeffer's era; it's a part of the current Canadian experience as well. The fantasy cycle not only fuels the *circulation of the saints* in the wider church, it can also fuel certain kinds of pioneer church planting. One planter suggested that for the good of the Canadian church,

> *"... we don't need the cycle of: get hired by a church, get discontented with the church, and plant your own church. We need something fresh..."*

We need a new way of living out our lives together. Decades of deconstructing the church has set the stage for pioneer church planting. It has created widespread anticipation and dreaming. What we need now is for God to raise up imaginative and hopeful revolutionaries who can point the way forward. We need them to be hopeful and imaginative in their dreaming and in their building. We also need them to stay connected to reality as they work.

As our study indicated, pioneer church planting doesn't have to become an endless loop through the fantasy cycle. People can and do learn to balance hopes and dreams with the demands of reality. But this is a significant challenge. So how did they do it?

I believe there are three basic lenses that participants in this study used to correct their tendencies toward fantasy. For one, pioneer church planters are prone to fantasy visions of the nature of the church. The corrective is a more robust and reality-based vision of the nature of the church. Second, pioneer church planters are prone to fantasies about how people are transformed in community. The corrective for this is a robust and reality-based vision of discipling. And finally, pioneer church planters are prone to fantasies about themselves as leaders. The corrective for this is a robust and reality-based vision of leadership. So let's take a look through each of these correctives lenses to see how they help us avoid blurry images of the fantasy church.

A Clearer Vision of the Church

There is neither time nor space here to develop a full-fledged ecclesiology. This study can only point to the fact that church planters need a good one. Planters need to know what they mean when they say the word "church." Several participants expressed this sentiment. One said:

"Some of the people I see out there have a very low ecclesiology. They say things like, 'We've just got to get back to the book of Acts.' To me, that view of church lacks the complexity of the problems of our world. Unfortunately, that's just not going to work. It's like the difference between being a child and being an adult. When children are small, things have to be simple in order to understand. As you grow into adulthood your perceptions become more

complex. Churches that start with and maintain a simplistic, childlike view from their inception never become mature because they always hold to a simplistic view of the church."

Distorted, overly simplistic fantasy images of the church are no help at all; in many cases they can actually be lethal. That's why it is imperative that planters immerse themselves in meaningful conversations about the church. Many pioneer planters focus on developing skills in community engagement. After all, this is where the missionary rubber meets the road. Unfortunately, there often isn't as much emphasis on developing skills in group self-reflection and self-awareness. Self-reflection and self-awareness are powerful corrective lenses. My friend Geoff Holsclaw once said, "Theology without mission is daydreaming; mission without theology is sleepwalking." Pioneer planters need to work out a balance of communal practice and communal reflection. They need to uncover the principles that guide their practice. They also need to uncover their assumptions and explanations of how their church functions and test them against reality.

This isn't a job for planters alone. Denominations and networks can also play an important role in encouraging thoughtful reflection. We need to ask questions like, "What is happening in our own churches?" and "What are we learning about the church together?" What's required to get us moving in this direction is for denominations to begin seeing themselves as communities of practice rather than simply credentialing bodies and legal umbrellas. Denominations are uniquely positioned to be doing practical research, both formally and informally on the work their churches are already doing. Without personalized and self-reflective inquisitiveness, the church in Canada will continue to lack true understanding of itself. And lack of genuine self-understanding readily gives way to fantasy.

If denominations would like to move toward being communities of practice and self-reflection, I think they will need to shape their question-asking in at least two directions. The first would be to ask, "Among our churches, what is and isn't working?" The second would be to ask, "How do we define 'working'?" These questions inform one another, and asking these questions together can help denominations avoid fantasy.

By asking, "What's working?" denominations can go beyond simply celebrating when a church plant succeeds to finding principles. Celebrating success is great but finding principles is better—they lead to communal self-understanding. They lead to better future attempts at church planting. "What isn't working?" is an equally valid question but it can be a little tougher to ask. While the temptation to gloss over or ignore when things don't work out is understandable it is also deeply unhelpful. Nevertheless, denominations can learn just as much from non-continuing plants as continuing plants. Unfortunately, there is often hand-wringing and embarrassment associated with church plants that close and so denominations are often reluctant to investigate. In economic terms, this is called risk aversion and it can lead to protracted periods of stagnation. In order to ask both questions well, denominations need to examine the cultural mechanisms that create shame and embarrassment. Denominational cultures that have little to no capacity for risk are in trouble—more on this in later chapters.

Denominations and networks that want to become communities of healthy practice for pioneer church planters will also need to define what is meant by "working." Definitions of success are a major component of ecclesiology. Definitions of success drive expectations—they are the plumb lines used for building. They can reveal whether a work is off track or on course. They can even show whether or not a church plant is actually over. By bringing these definitions to the surface and talking openly about them, denominations can not only become more truthful in their self-reflection, but safeguard their perceptions of reality in the Canadian mission field.

A Clearer Vision of Discipling

Pioneer church planters are prone to fantasies about how people are transformed in community. The corrective to this is a robust and reality-based vision of discipling. One planter put it this way:

> *"No matter how radical your church planting ideas are, no matter how different you think you are from the traditional church, you've got to remember that people are still people."*

Radical church planting ideas do not necessarily lead to changed lives—people are still people. People carry with them all of the hope and all of the fallenness that has alternately buoyed and sunk the church for centuries. They bring these not only to traditional churches, established churches, dying churches, thriving churches, and church plants, but yes even to radical new models of church. If planters want a reality-based relationship with people then they need to take steps to understand the task of discipling *their* people; not a fantasy people, or the people that "should be" joining their church, but the people that are there already. A robust and reality-based vision of discipling means that planters must have a vision for how a person in *their* neighbourhood, who currently lives their life outside the kingdom will: 1) connect to life in the church plant, 2) eventually get connected to Jesus, 3) discover belonging in the life of the church, 4) be taught to obey all that Jesus commanded, and 5) share in the plant's work in the neighbourhood. Pioneer church plants that had a detailed plan for discipleship—or at least had a mechanism to develop a plan for discipleship—tended to fare better than those that didn't. Anything less than a detailed plan for discipleship invites fantasy.

Here's how to start: begin with the end in mind. This means being clear about what you as a planter hope will result in people's lives as they live among you. Here are some helpful questions to get you started:

- What kind of people are most likely to share life with us?

- What will they be looking for? (Lots of people join church plants for less than ideal reasons like: time, location, it feels new, liking the music, or liking the preaching.)

- Are we happy that they will be looking for those things or do we need to work at adjusting their expectations?

- What condition are they likely to arrive in?

- Is there anything specific about our context that needs to be kept in mind?

- What local factors shape the starting point of people here?

- When it comes to life transformation, what do we *expect* to see?

- What do we *hope* to see?

- What practices will we have to engage in regularly so that discipling conditions are ideal?

- If we want our people to obey Jesus, what will they need to know about Him first?

- What will they need to know second, etc.?

- How will we figure out what actually happens in people after they've lived life among us for a while?

- What will we do if we don't like what we find?

- How will we communicate what we expect to see in a clear enough way that people will quickly get what we mean by a "disciple"?

These kinds of questions are vital. They force our hand and make us think more clearly and intentionally about our expectations and what we're doing. If churches are clear and intentional about what they expect, if they are clear and intentional about what they communicate, if they are clear and intentional about how they intend to figure out what their life together actually produces, then fantasy will have a really hard time taking root.

A Clearer Vision of Leadership

Pioneer church planters are prone to fantasies about themselves as leaders. The corrective for this is a robust and reality-based vision of leadership. How planters imagine themselves as leaders is absolutely vital in breaking the fantasy cycle.

Here's a personal story: what I have learned about and wrestled with most in this study is a deep sense of shame when things haven't work out for my friends, especially the ones featured in the documentary. I have been personally haunted by the fact that people I thought would be making the lifelong leadership journey with me have dropped off the path. I found myself delaying this project because of worry about what I might uncover. Some of these plants closed on my watch as a denominational leader. One of them actually closed while I was the chair of their board. Most of these stories are the stories of close personal friends. The experience of sitting down with them and talking directly and in depth about what happened has been thrilling and heartbreaking, often at the same time. When things haven't worked out for my friends I have felt responsible. I have wished I had done more. I have come to the point of asking myself, what if my best is not nearly good enough? Would another leader have done a better job?

Thoughts like these suggest that I too have a fantasy picture of my own leadership. When pioneer church plants and planters don't make it, I take a hit to my personal identity. The church planting environment I set out to create was supposed to be different! I promised to make it easier for new planters than it was for me. I was supposed to be a different *kind* of leader. The underlying expectation in my own leadership is that everyone will succeed all of the time. This kind of thinking is what my friend Al Doseger calls "building a fence without a gate." It's fantasy with no escape. Somewhere along the line, I replaced the easy yoke of Jesus with someone else's burden.

This was an important realization for me in this project. And it wasn't magic—it was because I asked questions in a systematic and plodding way. It was because I asked these questions in community with others. It was because I engaged in self-reflection. The act of facing reality burns away the mists of fantasy and helps us see more clearly.

A corrective to fantasy pictures of leadership is to remember the primary task of a Christian leader. A Christian leader's primary task is not to be successful, but to be faithful to God. This is an important starting point. Beginning here makes us much more responsive to what God wants to accomplish in and through our leadership. Starting anywhere else takes us into a fantasy land. The process of living out our calling in leadership—just like living out any other calling in the body of the church—is first and foremost a process of sanctification. God wants to sanctify us in our ministry. Successful use of skills will always be secondary. God's primary concern is on deepening our character, and *not* simply ensuring that we're meeting some kind of skill standards.

Look at how God has worked through leaders in the Bible. What do you see in His modus operandi? What do you see in the stories of Abraham, Isaac, Jacob, Moses, David, and Peter for instance? Do you see success? Abraham short circuited a promise. Isaac failed to bless the "right" son. Jacob stole what he wanted. Moses didn't get to see the Promised Land. David was a man of blood. Peter often needed three cracks at it before he understood what was going on. These aren't success stories.

They are stories of a journey with God, a journey in which He disciplines you, frustrates you, forgives you, and shows grace and patience toward you. The aim is a life lived with God—not the achievement of a set of S.M.A.R.T. goals. To neglect this truth is to leave yourself open to fantasies about who God is and what He wants.

Another way for leaders to begin thinking more clearly about themselves and their roles is to guard their hearts against comparison. If leadership is primarily about the character of the leader, then bringing someone else's story into the mix serves no good purpose. As a leader, comparing yourself to others cuts in two ways. The first is through negative comparison.

I noticed during my interviews that a lot of planters brought up what other leaders thought about them; they seemed to feel under attack. And yet, I often couldn't find any evidence of how these "attacks" actually made any difference in their community. These so-called attacks seemed to be limited to mere disapproval or a sense of other leaders just not "getting it." Preoccupation with the opinion of others does little to help you live more fully and faithfully into the work that God has given you to do. If, as a leader, you find yourself fantasizing about how tragically misunderstood you are, or how courageous you are for going against the flow, pay attention. Assigning blame to others and declaring your own innocence is called scapegoating and it's the oldest trick in the fantasy play book. It will do you no good.

The second way comparison cuts leaders is that it can cause you to become jealous of other leaders. Jealousy leads to all sorts of distorted thinking. The truth is that God asked *you* to serve here—and not someone else. Own that. Live into that. Wishing you were somewhere else, or someone else, doesn't lead to clear thinking—it leads to toxic fantasy. Unhelpful comparisons often make you feel alone—even though it's an artificial kind of alone. Allowing jealousy to take root will push you outside the safety of your support community. Keep your leadership story your own.

Finally, as a leader, remember that you are a part of a body. Your work as a planter is not up to you only. That's what all those other people gathered around you are for. In my experience, many planters lack the patience required to share their vision clearly so that others are able to meaningfully participate and share responsibility. Communication is a skill. Communication is also an ongoing exercise in patience. If you lack the will to communicate or the patience to do it well, you will find yourself alone. Ephesians 4:12 reminds us that the primary task of church leadership is to equip *others* for works of service. Equipping others for works of service is a time-consuming investment of energy. Some planters feel it would be simpler to do things themselves and simply to invite other people to gather and watch. This might make for compelling theatre, but it doesn't do much for your long-term prospects of living or surviving as a body of Christ.

Here are some helpful questions to ask yourself about... yourself!

- Do I understand my own motivations for planting in the first place?

- Do I have a sense of what God would like to teach me through my life as leader in this next season?

- Where does my authority come from?

- Does fear of failure drive or paralyze me?

- Do I engage in unhelpful fantasies about how awesome I am because I am a church planter?

- Am I aware of my own weaknesses as a leader?

- Am I aware of my strengths?

- When I'm around other pastors how do I feel?

- Do I have a real plan to mitigate my weaknesses?

- Does anyone else know what is actually going on in my heart?

- Do I have a few older, wiser voices that I depend on for their wealth of experience?

- Am I tempted to keep secrets from people?

- Do I share the burden of my vision or do I imagine myself heroically taking it on alone?

Regularly asking these kinds of questions can help you cultivate a clear mind when it comes to leadership.

The fantasy cycle is real. It has to be acknowledged and talked about if your church plant has any hope of not being caught up in it. Fantasies always promise more than they deliver. As your plant struggles to remain in contact with reality, it is imperative that you keep your collective wits about you as a church plant. Be aware that the fantasy cycle will challenge your most cherished hopes and dreams, and be ready for it. It will call into question the very things that make up your identity. It will claim you and your plant if you do not collectively develop the language, the conservation mechanisms, and the structures required to keep in touch with reality. Talking openly and honestly about your expectations both as individuals and as a group are vital to your survival. Be clear about and engage in clarifying conversations about the nature of your church. Do this inside and outside your church plant. Get into a network and learning community. Be clear about what you expect your life together as a plant to produce in terms of disciples. Revisit these expectations regularly. Adjust as necessary. Be open and honest with yourself and others about who you are as a leader. Beating the fantasy cycle takes clear-headedness, courage, and an openness to talk.

5

Watch Your Heart

Planters who watched their hearts did much better over the long run than those who left their character issues unaddressed.

"I think we go into church planting with the idea that this will be enjoyable. I don't think anyone goes into it thinking that this will be a process of holiness. But that's what it is—a process of holiness."

Pioneer church planting is a process of holiness. It represents a chance to step out in faith, a chance to willingly engage in sacrifice, and a chance to see God at work right in the middle of your life. These are all part of the process of sanctification. But, as with any human journey, results may vary.

In our study, planters who were able to watch their hearts did much better than those who left their character issues unaddressed. This is not meant to insinuate that the church plant closures were caused by character issues; church plants close for a variety of reasons. And yet, a significant number of planters told me that character was something they wished they had paid closer attention to during the planting process. This regret was shared across the board. Leaders of continuing and non-continuing churches alike wished they had watched their hearts a little more. Since this was a common feature of planting in our study, let's take a closer look at issues of the heart and character in planting.

Let's start by talking about the importance of character. Jesus warned us that "a good man brings good things out of the good stored up in his heart, and an evil man brings evil things out of the evil stored up in his heart" (Luke 6:45). Church planting, if it accomplishes anything, accomplishes bringing the things hidden in a planter's hearts into reality. Character matters. Character matters because our internal world fuels who we are and what we do. Character is our moral, emotional, and spiritual substance. Character affects who we imagine we are. Character colours how we see the world around us. And the best news of all? In Christ's hands, our character doesn't have to be a static state. God can do more with us than simply forgive us. In the skillful hands of God, we can experience all kinds of freedom and transformation at the deepest levels of who we are. God's work can enable us to approach life from an increasingly Christ-like place.

Okay, so it's important for a planter to watch their heart and give themselves over to the work of God, but how does that directly affect church planting outcomes? Well, for starters, the internal world of the heart plays a huge role in shaping the culture of the churches planters start. As Simon Sinek is famous for saying, "People don't buy what you do; they buy why you do it." The condition of a planter's heart shapes why they do what they do. What they do shapes what they become. Here's where it gets tricky: the reasons why planters plant in the first place, especially the less than noble ones, never seem to make it onto the church website or the felt banner behind the drum set. But just because they aren't made public doesn't make them any less powerful in shaping what church plants do together and who they become together.

Most participants told me that it took years for their plants to come to any true understanding of who they actually were. In the timeline of a church plant's life, by the time the church is able to articulate such things, serious layers of cultural cement will have already set. A planter may find that they have accumulated a hodgepodge of good and bad materials in the foundations of their church culture. If, as a planter, you keep a sharp eye out, you'll notice this immediately and have the chance to take a jackhammer to the weak spots and fix your foundation. On the other hand, if you don't pay attention, all will be revealed when a stiff wind blows or the waters rise.

Since it's not uncommon for a church plant to accumulate good and bad reasons for existing, based on the motivations of the planter, it would be helpful to do some reflecting on how to tell the difference between the two. First, let's look at the bad reasons. What does it look like and how can you tell?

Hey, Look at Me!

A common and powerful motivator for a person to church plant can be to gain the approval of others. But just because it's powerful doesn't make it healthy. Here's what one participant said about their motivation:

> *"Being young and being somewhat insecure, I wanted somebody's stamp of approval. That's the dark part."*

Church planting, especially in the early stages, can be all about the church planter. This can seem unavoidable since at the earliest stages, the planter is literally the only thing that actually exists. It's just you, your calling, and your idea. People will have to decide if they will join you, your calling, and your idea, and make it into something more. Many will make the choice to join you because they like you. This feels good. But if it develops into your primary motivation to plant and their primary motivation to stay then you're all in trouble. Churches *can* continue on this foundation for remarkable periods of time. One planter described his experience this way:

> *"Early on, I developed a bit of a Messiah complex. I was the one hanging with all the hard to reach people. I was the one doing all the preaching. I was the one leading the vision and*

mission. I was the one pushing the boundaries... This can last for about a year and then it's either going to be your family, or yourself, or something else that is going to fall apart. It becomes a 'this is my ministry' mentality over and against the church as a whole."

As Christians, we know that the job of "Messiah" has already been filled. We also know that a healthy church is a body of believers, not a one-person show. None of us would ever consciously build a church around ourselves. But despite all of this—it still happens. And when it does happen, it's an exhausting experience. It's not good for planters physically, emotionally, or spiritually, and in some cases it perversely twists their ego.

Here's why you don't want to build a church plant with this mentality. Your approval rating, as a leader, is going to fluctuate over time. Sometimes as a leader you will need to make hard or unpopular decisions. If your ego requires that you be universally loved and celebrated all the time, you will be tempted or unable to make healthy decisions when they are needed. Alternatively, if your church thrives on constant and unending access to you and you alone, then the culture you create will either artificially limit growth or eventually kill you. Both aren't great for your long-term prospects. Church planters and congregations who are able to recognize the signs of *Hey, Look at Me!* and push back against them do better in the long run than those that can't.

I'll Show Them!

Another unstable heart motivation is to plant a church as a statement to the world. This one is particularly intoxicating for those attempting to plant a church that is a little out of the ordinary. The idea of pushing boundaries or being "on the edge" can lead to some very unhealthy results. One planter admitted:

"[My church planting idea] was birthed out of an unhealthy drive. Having success in my early ministry sort of made me

arrogant. My thought was, 'I am going to do this better than any other church.'"

Some of the planters I talked to seemed to take a certain amount of pride in the fact that they were almost universally misunderstood:

"I am a member of a denomination and they don't want anything to do with me, basically, because what I do is just too weird for them."

Others took unhealthy pride in their desire to pay attention to an overlooked people group in society: the poor and disenfranchised, angry young sons and daughters of evangelicalism (the "dones"), the nones, or some misunderstood artistic community. I call this phenomenon the "heroic alienation" narrative. Stories told in this way have an almost romantic quality to them. They lend their teller a kind of instant moral credibility. The pioneer planter is cast as the alienated hero who ventures out into the world, misunderstood and alone, willing to give it all as they love the hard to love and the easily ignored. Interestingly, at least for the churches in this study, they weren't really stretching the truth. Many of the 19 churches were working with people whom the church in Canada seemed to be ignoring. The danger in this motivation is the way it can feed the ego. It can place you far above other Christians who work with what you consider to be an "easy to reach" group.

Not only is the heroic alienation narrative profoundly toxic for the planter, but it can prematurely end the plant. There are several ways this can happen. First, nurturing a sense of heroic alienation can artificially isolate you from the broader church community and its collective wisdom. It can make you imagine enemies or criticism where they may not exist. It can make you immune to communal wisdom because "no one could possibly understand what it's like to do what I do." Isolation can hamper your ability to access vital denominational resources. If your default setting is always to assume that you're different and "nothing that works anywhere else could possibly work here," you will be perpetually stuck re-inventing the wheel, alone. It can also hamper your access to resources in the broader network. Gatherings of pioneer church planters that nurture a sense of heroic alienation will become competitive. In these arenas, the competition may not be about whose church is bigger but whose context is tougher. Second, heroic alienation can transform the people you are sent to serve from actual people into symbols of your own fearlessness. This view of people is deeply toxic and unsustainable. Church planters and congregations who are able to recognize and address the signs of *I'll Show You!* and push back against them do better in the long run than those that don't.

Building with Better

So, how do we find our way toward good and sturdy motivations for church planting? Put simply, the purest possible motivation for planting is a faithful obedience to God as He asks you to pour yourself into establishing a healthy church. No more, no less. While that is a simple sentence to write, when it comes to the human heart nothing is ever that simple. One planter really wanted to impress the importance of this on future planters:

> *"Check your motives, your attitudes, and your heart. There are a lot of things that can stand between you and loving God and loving others. That isn't something I saw years ago. It turns out that church planting was also about me. I was being sought by God along with the least, the lost, and the last."*

This wasn't a trite statement. This was hard-won advice. Church planting can be a process of holiness, but it takes a concerted and conscious effort to see it that way. Building with better materials means we'll need to keep a couple of things in mind.

The first is to begin the work of self-awareness even before starting to plant. Wisdom would suggest only proceeding with a plant once you are fully convinced that God has asked you to do it. That means taking time: taking time to fast, taking time to pray, taking time to listen to the wisdom of others. It means

56 | Watch Your Heart

taking time to search your heart and ask yourself some good questions:

- What is this really about for me?

- Do I find myself attracted to planting for reasons other than pleasing God and serving others?

- Does my mind often move to fantasies about something other than simply establishing a healthy church?

- Do those fantasies include recognition or vindication in some way?

- Do I have a hidden agenda here?

- Can I say with deep confidence that this is something that God wants me to do?

Key Questions

The second is to make a thorough search of your heart an ongoing personal discipline. Church planting shouldn't be done alone. You are going to need a deep and constant connection to God. Take regular time to place your heart and life in front of God. You could consider David's famous words as a place to start:

"Search me, God, and know my heart; test me and know my anxious thoughts. See if there is any offensive way in me, and lead me in the way everlasting" (Psalm 139:23-24).

You may find that God is especially willing to answer prayers like this. Sometimes He'll answer by placing people in your life that ask tough questions. Let them in. Let them do their work. Invite them to drill down into your motivations. Ask them to listen closely to the stories you tell and ask you questions about what is driving you.

The third is to learn how to lead your community in this process. There is tremendous power in communal question-asking. Don't be afraid to lead your church into the same kind of self-examination that you yourself are engaging in. While it may make some uncomfortable, over the long haul, you're going to need to surround yourself with people that can search their hearts along with you. Here's what one planter advised:

"You're going to need ridiculous faith, constant patience, and to surround yourself with kind people."

That sounds like a good recipe.

Here are some questions to help you get started with communal heart searching:

- What are some the best reasons you have for wanting to be a part of this church?

- What are some reasons that you might not be so proud of?

- When we talk about what it is we are doing what words do we often choose?

- Do those words sound accurate?

- Do they point to some other hidden agenda?

- Is there a specific church or type of church that we regularly define ourselves over and against?

- Do you share the same sense of ownership that I do?

- Or are you simply coming to "my" church?

If you ask one another these kinds of questions on a more or less regular basis you can ensure that hidden motivations don't stay permanently hidden, but can be exposed and challenged.

It's vitally important that planters and churches take seriously the way that church planting can be a process of holiness. It's important to take seriously the fact that God cares more about who you become, together, rather than what you produce. Doing this involves understanding and exposing faulty motivations that can cloud your collective church planting vision. Look at your own heart carefully as a planter, both before you start and while you're in full swing. Your older brothers and sisters—the leaders of these continuing and not continuing pioneer churches—all wished that they had taken this a little more seriously. It's only wise for you to heed their warnings and learn from their experience.

6

Be Ready for Growing Pains

Planters who unapologetically pursued becoming a healthy church did better than planters who were motivated negatively to not become a traditional church.

"Okay, it's time. We've got to grow up and stop pretending we don't like committees."

In the church planting stories I heard, planters commonly experienced hesitation around what they termed "growing up." For them, "growing up" meant developing more formal structures in their churches. So what was the big deal? Well, more formal structures somehow seemed to be synonymous with "becoming like other churches."

We need to remember here that for pioneer church plants, success is two-fold: they must not only succeed in what they do, but they must also find a new way to do it. To succeed at one and fail at the other is not success at all. It can be a difficult balancing act. Developing more structures, agreeing to processes, and even writing stuff down can seem antithetical to much of a church plant's basic identity. Creative churches don't develop policies. Organic churches don't need to organize committees. Relational churches don't need conflict resolution processes. Spirit-led churches don't need to write things down or have board meetings. You name the identity category, and structure seems to be its opposite.

The churches in our study generally responded to the need to "grow up" in one of two ways. The first was to develop a begrudging and ironic relationship with organizing themselves. The second was to delay and avoid increased organization like the plague. Churches in this study that were eventually able to plug their noses and take their medicine did better in the long run than churches that stubbornly resisted it. These churches might not have enjoyed the process but they saw the creation of structures as an important developmental milestone.

We can't go so far as to say that a total lack of structure ever ended a church plant—because a complete lack of structure simply doesn't exist. Any community of people that regularly share life together, develop common practices, and form a common identity have at least some structures. These structures may all be informal, written down on the back of a napkin so to speak, but they are structures all the same. The question for a church plant isn't whether or not to have structures, but about how much is necessary and how formal it should be. Here's one participant's take:

> *"There are things that are intrinsically important. It's great to be organic, it's great to have the environment right, but sooner or later you are going to need some structure."*

This eventual need for structure popped up in many of the stories I heard. Most of the planters sensed that they needed it. Interestingly, the signal for more structure rarely came from denominational expectations or some other external source. It came from people within the plant itself.

A growing sense of a need for structure seems like an important milestone in the proper development of a church plant. None of the plants that sensed that it was the time to "grow up" and develop structures regretted their decision; it was a universally positive experience. Even those that sensed a need and waited for a long time before implementing structure had a positive experience—their only regret was waiting so long. However there was a third category that seemed to hold out to the point of danger, a decision that really seemed to impact their health. Why would you ignore your own instincts? Perhaps it was the fantasy cycle. Maybe avoiding structure is a way to hit the snooze button and keep the dream alive— a dream in which your church is so clearly and purely conceived, so powerfully lead, and so richly populated with committed people that will naturally, voluntarily, and consistently do all that is necessary to ensure the smooth running of the community, that structure is never necessary. Perhaps choosing structure feels like letting a dream die for certain churches—maybe it feels like failing as a pioneer.

These are the growing pains of pioneer church planting. Developing structures seems to be important and necessary... eventually. And yet, developing structures can also feel like letting go of some the magic of the early days and becoming like every other church. In the rest of this chapter we're going to explore two things. The first is to look at what our planters did to get over their discomfort with structure. The second is to discover what benefits they experienced through improving and deepening their structures.

The Tyranny of the Urgent

Perhaps the greatest hurdle to "growing up" for planters is learning how to get over the discomfort of putting energy into structures. Structures take serious investments of time and energy and yet they seldom feel urgent. They are important, but they frequently get put off until later. One church plant in the study took nearly ten years to form a board made up of people from within the church. In the early days, when finding good leaders in the plant was harder, they found people outside the church to lend a hand. It was a good idea at the time. Unfortunately, it also took the pressure off the planter and the people to develop a leadership culture themselves. Sometimes, pressure can be a good thing—just ask a diamond! Unfortunately, this church plant now faces an uphill battle because its people are in the habit of leaving leadership to others. In the study, I also found a few church plants that were heavily dependent on outside sponsors for a majority of their finances. Again, taking the pressure off your people can feel like a good idea, and maybe in the early days it is. However, as a long-term strategy it can lead to serious problems.

Healthy churches are made up of people with a sense of collective ownership. They are generous, they practice sacrificial love, and they have learned to re-organize their whole lives (including their finances) around kingdom priorities. Pressure is often needed to make diamonds of this quality—it may not be pleasant but it is important. Strategies that circumvent natural pressure and support the habit of putting off developmental milestones can negatively impact a church plant's health. One planter described the practice of putting off developing structures as creating a "prolonged adolescence." Growing up isn't easy. It sometimes means doing things that you don't want to do, or investing in things that you don't enjoy. It can even mean intentionally exposing yourself in ways that feel mildly dangerous at the time. In the end, these growing pains are what produce maturity.

The Power of Writing It Down

Another practice planters mentioned as a helpful part of building structure was putting things down on paper:

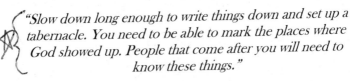

> *"Slow down long enough to write things down and set up a tabernacle. You need to be able to mark the places where God showed up. People that come after you will need to know these things."*

There is a peculiar power, at least in Western culture, in putting things down on paper. The children of Israel used to pile up rocks to mark the places where God showed up. Westerners use piles of words. Marking our places of encounter with God has several benefits.

The first is that the writing process enables you as a planter to slow down and clarify. Church life can be hectic, moving from experience to experience. It's easy to lose track of the bigger picture. The gift of writing is that it forces you to slow down. Writing cannot be rushed. It is a process of sifting, refining, and polishing. Thoughts and ideas that live in the oral tradition of your church are powerfully transformed when they are written down—they crystallize; they become more material. Writing can lend new weight to the words you use to describe yourselves as a church. The written word can also feel contractual. If you are struggling with wider ownership in the church, writing things down can help. Here's how one planter described the process of writing down the church's values:

"There was a stronger sense of vision and purpose and 'this is who we are.' You know, you are welcome to go somewhere else, but this is what God has asked us to do, where He asked us to do it. These were foundational statements that we probably didn't make and if we did make them they were pretty soft."

The written word, because it feels contractual in our Western culture, can help a church define expectations, roles, and develop a deeper sense of ownership.

The Power of Regular Dialogue

A third practice planters learned to value was regular, structured dialogue. Some booked regular time for group reflection into their church calendar. One plant hosted a monthly gathering to reflect on their own values. Together as a plant they looked at what they were doing and asked, how does this fit with our values? This structured practice did several things for them. The first was that it ensured they weren't spending energy on things that didn't matter. It gave them constant reality checks. The regularity of the conversation meant that people deeply understood and practiced the values. They could see the connection between what they valued and how they lived together. It was powerful. Structured dialogue can do a lot to create a sense of continuity and community. One planter put it this way:

> *"You don't just launch once and you're done. For the first four years, it feels like you launch every year. There is lot of come and go, and that takes a lot of energy and planning."*

It's important to remember that regular dialogue takes energy and planning. It can sometimes feel like work, but it's worth it. In one planter's words:

> *"I would have thought that strategizing was the best way to shape an ethos, but it's not. Self-reflection and organizational reflection were two of the most powerful things that we ever did."*

In this planter's church plant they planned their dialogue on a yearly cycle. Every year they agreed to blow up last year's plan, if necessary, and start over. In March, the church would begin reflecting on their structure. They would reflect on the types of people who were currently a part of the church and what they were doing together as a church. They would then evaluate whether or not what they were doing suited the type of people currently represented in the congregation. In June, they released everyone for their ministry positions and began planning adjustments for the fall. By September they put those adjustments in place. Said the planter:

> *"Our structure and our ethos and those kinds of things did shift and change. And yet, I can't remember a time when it was chaotic, hurtful, or when people got left in the dust."*

It was this process that enabled this church to preserve a sense of calm and continuity even though they underwent several major changes—the kind of major changes that could have easily made it impossible for the plant to continue. They survived a change in neighbourhood, changes in the kinds of people they reached, changes in roles, changes in expectations, and several changes in ministry direction. Structured conversation is what enabled them to adjust and to be responsive to who, when, and where they were at any given time. It's what helped them not develop fantasy attachments to the way things "used to be."

Okay, so structure can be a good thing—something worth investing in. Now let's turn our attention to the kinds of things that good structure actually helps plants to do.

Spiritual Health

Spiritual health is vital to the growth and sustainability of a church plant. Structure, believe it or not, can play a major role in promoting spiritual health. Throughout the history of the church, we can see time and again that a deeper connection to God can come as much from spontaneous sacred experiences as it can from disciplined practice. Discipleship should consist of things like life together and "as you go" kinds of experiences *and* things like teaching, shared life rhythms, structured relationships, group learning, and group practices. This isn't an either/or reality. Structure doesn't have to be antithetical to your spiritual identity. Listen to these comments from one planter:

> *"We're at that teenage stage where we are finding our voice. So, we're putting systems in place for our own discipline, we're starting to put our elders into place. We've had lots of vine, but it's time to get some trellis in place. And a lot of people are happy to see these things being put into place."*

Structures can actually make people happy! How is that possible? Well, when structures develop in pace with the spiritual growth of your congregation, a good thing is made even better. Structures can actually deepen growth—not by replacing growth but by benefiting what is there. Structures can play a vital role not only in spiritual growth, but also in healing. See this planter's experience:

"One of the things I realized was that the woundedness that enabled me to start this church was not enough to see it flourish. If I had just lived in the woundedness I would be missing a major piece. I think you have to experience the woundedness and know you can create a worship space that includes other wounded people—but you have to call them to something else. You can't leave them there too long. You have to take everyone's energy and pain and move it somewhere else."

Structures do wonders in helping churches call their people toward deeper healing. As one church described it, *"eventually you need to transition from being an E.R. (Emergency Room) to being a rehab centre."* This is an instructive metaphor. An E.R. and a rehab centre care for patients at very different points in their recovery. Each has a unique environment through which they apply their particular brand of healing. An E.R. is an environment for people who are in crisis. A rehab centre is an environment for people to heal once the crisis has passed. An E.R. is about pain relief. A rehab centre may need to cause some pain in order to facilitate long-term healing. Yet, complete healing requires both environments and both approaches to medicine. And it is the structure of the hospital that helps people find their way between these worlds, a structure that makes the referrals, schedules the appointments, provides the gentle reminders, and tracks progress. Churches need to invest in structures if they want to promote full spiritual healing. They need ways to assess, track, and encourage their people to keep going on their journey to full recovery.

The first step toward churches becoming good facilitators of spiritual health is developing a fuller definition of spiritual health. Some churches in the study seemed too easily satisfied when people simply felt safe in their church. This is important, no doubt, but feeling safe is only the beginning of spiritual health! Churches must ask deeper questions. Here are some questions that could encourage some more helpful conversations around spiritual health in your plant:

- Do we have a clear and full picture of what a healthy Christian looks like?

- Is this picture discussed and understood by all?

- Does our picture include not only the absence of pain but full and active use of all of our God-given spiritual capacities?

- Are those spiritual capacities employed mostly for personal use or do they benefit others?

- Does our picture of spiritual health include actively reorganizing how we live around kingdom values?

- Do our personal priorities reflect kingdom ones?

- Are we fully engaged in the historic Christian practices that promote ongoing health?

- Do we make Christian community a priority?

- Are we actively involved in being discipled?

- Are we discipling others?

- Do we pray?

- Do we fast?

- Do we practice generosity as a lifestyle?

- Are our lives shaped by Scripture?

- By solitude?

- Do we regularly show care to people in need?

- Do we show care for creation?

- Is our life anchored by a deep sense of God's love and delight in us?

- How will we take stock of what's going on in our lives?

Churches that make asking questions like these a regular and normal part of life together will do better in terms of spiritual health than churches that don't.

Stability

Stability is an important factor in the long-term health of church plants. Church plants can be a whirlwind of activity, especially in the early days. Ideas and possibilities all fly a mile a minute in a thousand different directions. Stability is needed to smooth out the extremes and proceed in a discernable direction. Structures—meaning frameworks that promote repetition and predictability—are what make stability possible.

The first advantage of stability is that it enables you to understand your context. Getting to know a neighbourhood takes time. One planter told me that it took between four and five years for his plant to make some of their most important connections and relationships in their neighbourhood. Trust takes time to form. Word takes time to spread. If you're in a rush or you flit from one idea to the next, certain aspects of your neighbourhood will remain inaccessible to you. If you want in on that action, you'll need to develop structures that promote stability.

The second advantage of stability is that it permits you to see the kind of transformation that can take years to realize. This long-term transformation is revealed in all kinds of ways in a church plant. In the case of vision and values, one planter told me that it took years for some people in their church to understand its vision. Several others said that it took years for their church plants to understand and clearly articulate their real values. These planters were quick to mention that writing things down and regularly re-visiting and updating what was written down can really help with this process. In the case of discipleship, planters told me that consistently and repetitively practicing the same things year after year is what it really takes to disciple people. In some cases, it will take years or even decades, to start seeing results. Helping people subvert the fantasy cycle and begin engaging with a real community, with real human beings, and with a realistic picture of themselves and their context takes time. If these are the kinds of things you want in your church plant then you'll need to develop structures that promote stability.

So, in the church planting stories shared with me, planters commonly experienced hesitation around "growing up." Growing up meant developing more formal structures in their church. Churches that were eventually able to overcome their hesitation around structure and process did better in the long run than churches that stubbornly resisted. Churches that were able to overcome their hesitation never regretted it. These churches learned to resist the temptation to put off developing structure in favour of more urgent concerns. They learned the power of writing things down to help solidify and crystallize what they were doing. They also learned the power of regular dialogue. By booking this into the church calendar, they were able to remain flexible and keep pace with the changes in their neighbourhood and their people. Churches that valued and developed structure found that it helped them accomplish two very important things: first, they were able to promote and facilitate spiritual health in their people. Second, they gained a stability that unlocked deeper connections both to the neighbourhood and the lives of their own people.

7

Do You Know What Success Looks Like?

Plants that developed ways of building on success and adapting after failure did better than churches that refused to examine themselves according to any standards—even their own.

"One of the things I asked of my denomination was to leave us alone, and to let us do what we wanted to do. Looking back on it today, I think they should have said no. They should have let us move according to our vision, but we needed more guidance—especially when things were falling apart. But the thing is, when you're starting something like this, you think you know what you want. Denominations need to ask, 'Really? Do you really know what you want?' or 'You may know what you want. But do you know what you're going to get?'"

Getting what you want isn't always what you want. Many come to the church planting task with unhealthy or unhelpful standards of success. Most of us are happy to critique the classic definition of success: more butts, bucks, and buildings—and there is a lot to criticize in this definition. For starters, Jesus did not tell us to go into all the world and make attenders; he told us to make disciples. Counting heads on

Sunday morning doesn't tell you much about the state of people's lives. To those of us uncomfortable with the current definition of success, great! We're paying attention. There are serious problems with it. Everyone agreed? Good, motion carried. Now onto new business. Anybody have any ideas on what we should replace it with? Crickets...

While we're waiting I'm going to do something a bit risky and propose a possible definition of success. I hope you'll hear me out before you tear it to pieces. What if success was "being faithful to whatever it is that God asked you to do"? Too simple? Maybe. Hard to define? Possibly. Then again, maybe it's crazy enough to work. Here's my logic: given the complexity of the current Canadian reality, we can safely assume we're not all being sent out to do the same job. Some will be sent out to stabilize what already exists. Some will be sent out to repair. Some will be sent out to forge new ground. You know, different parts but one Spirit kinds of stuff. So, what if there wasn't one unifying definition of success for every church in every place? What if our definition of success is supposed to depend on the assignment we've been given? For instance, success in a conflicted church might mean a total focus on unity and conflict resolution. Numerical growth may not be part of the equation for a long time. It may even wind up being a distraction! Success in a complacent church may mean fostering holy discontent and discomfort—two things that can act as serious growth inhibitors! What if our definition of success changed as the people and the job did?

The job for pioneer churches, as we have mentioned already, is two-fold—they must not only succeed in what they do (plant a church), but they must also find a new way to be the church (a new kind of church). Let's take a closer look. Finding a "new way to be the church" means being the church in ways that actually tests the currently accepted definitions of church. That takes a willingness to courageously ask a ton of "What if?" questions. Success would also mean courageously attempting a lot of "What if?"-inspired plans. Succeeding at pioneer church planting also means actually planting a church. The "What if?" questions mentioned above need to be rooted and informed by the three basic functions of being a church, which are: 1) meaningfully living out the gospel in a context, 2) establishing an environment and practices that make spiritual health and spiritual growth likely for the people in that context, and 3) training people and sending them out to repeat the process.

If success means being faithful to whatever it is that God has asked you to do, then how do we measure our faithfulness? How do we avoid fooling ourselves? What I want to propose in the rest of this chapter are two ways that we can begin to measure faithfulness. These measures are meant to be performed regularly and to be tweaked as you go in order to accurately reflect your calling and your reality.

Doing What God Asked You to Do

The first way to measure the faithfulness of your community is to assess if you're doing the things God asked you to do. To do this you'll need to ask three questions: First, what does God want us to do? Second, what are we currently doing? Third, are we doing it well? Let's consider each of these in turn to see how this might work.

What does God want us to do? This is a powerful question. Powerful because it allows for our understanding of ourselves and of God to change. If asked collectively, it immediately invites the community to bring themselves in front of God, to bring their activities under His authority, to bring their priorities and preferences under His guidance, and to submit themselves to Him. It invites the group to expose their expectations and evaluate them in light of what God is doing. This process can be as simple as an invitation to an evening of prayer and listening. It can be as thoroughgoing as several weeks or even months of concerted prayer, fasting, talking, listening and imagining. Your context needs to shape your plan.

What are we currently doing? This means taking stock of the things that your community regularly puts its energies into. It is important that you not make this about what you wish you were doing, but stay focused on what is happening now. Take the advice of this planter:

> *"We didn't construct institutional pathways until we were certain where people were going to walk. University campuses have learned that they should never lay sidewalks until they have learned where students are going to walk. So look and see where the paths are and then you pave them."*

Here's a simple suggestion a few churches have tried: take an evening to sit down together and list all of the things that you regularly do as a church. Most churches, regardless of size or type, quickly find out they have a lot of stuff going on! It's a good realization to have. It can be an encouragement to those that might feel they're not doing enough. Ask yourselves if there are any major gaps in what you're doing. Are you overemphasizing one particular discipling task?

Are we doing what we're doing well? Here are some questions that can help you answer this question:

- How well are we doing at meaningfully living out the gospel in this context?

- Are people coming to faith?

- Are we living a life that looks like good news?

- Do the things we do make spiritual health and spiritual growth likely for our people?

- Do we actively measure that?

- Do we respond to what we find?

- Do we train people and then send them back out into the mission field?

It's important to do this honestly. Just because you have good ideas doesn't mean you are any good at pulling them off. Churches that are able to speak truthfully about their own effectiveness are much better at adapting to their context. Here's how one planter described their struggle:

> *"The worst part was I knew the concept was right. It was the best idea I'd ever had, and yet I couldn't make it work."*

It's important to be honest. It's also important not to do this work by yourself. You should avoid doing this stuff with a small group of leaders on your own—involve as many people as you can. This can help with honesty, and also help with communication. If you make discoveries as a tiny group of people it will be hard to translate that for the rest of the people in the church, even if communication is your strong suit. Instead, make every effort to make your discoveries together as a larger group. Any course correcting you need to do in response to what you learn will be so much easier if the whole group agrees together that changes are necessary.

Being Who You Said You Would Be

The second way to measure faithfulness is to assess if you're being the kind of church you said you would be. One of the ways a church plant can make this assessment is to develop a values-based evaluation. The basic idea is that you are successful if you are living into the unique values God has called you to have. To do this, you can follow a similar process to the one described in the previous section. You'll need to ask three questions: First, what kind of community has God ask us to be here? Second, how are we living into our values now? Third, are we living into those values consistently? Let's look at each of these in turn to see how this works.

What kind of community has God ask us to be here? It is important that church plants have a clear sense of their collective calling. Most callings either involve a particular place and people or a certain way of life. This can sometimes prove challenging for church plants to articulate, especially if they aren't used to writing things down. If you have never written down your sense of calling, a good place to start is to consider what makes your church plant unique—not better, unique. Your calling can also be found in the reasons you decided to plant in the first place. Was it a people group? Was it a specific way of being the church? Was it a specific place? Whatever it was, it needs to be talked about and written down. Callings are sacred. They are divine marching orders. God didn't give them to someone else; He gave them to you. That doesn't mean that you understand them perfectly or that they are for all time. But these callings are the most important place to start. They are also an important thing to re-evaluate on a regular basis. Here are some questions that might help:

- Do people in our church know what we mean when we describe our collective calling?

- Does the way we describe it still sound like good news to us?

- Does it sound like good news to our neighbours?

- Does it sound like a collection of Christian buzzwords or a foreign language?

- Is our current sense of our calling still connected to what He wants us to do?

How are we living into our values now? It's important to take stock. Look for the regular ways that your community lives out its declared values. How do they shake out in action? How do the community's values affect decisions that are made? How deeply do you share these values as a group? Take this planter's word for it:

"You can only go so far on your gut and your intuition. Time after time, I notice that people like me get ahead of the Spirit. Go slow. Go carefully. Even if your people are

agreeable, take the time to make sure that everyone is on the same page or at least the same chapter."

Don't move too quickly. Take your time. Don't quickly leap ahead. You should also turn your attention to your context: How are the values getting played out in your context now? Has anything changed in the environment that needs to be taken into consideration?

Are we consistently living into our values? Here are some questions to help guide your response:

- How does what we value help us to meaningfully live out the gospel in this context?

- Do our values interfere with this in any way?

- Are people coming to faith?

- Are we living a life that looks like good news?

- Do our values make spiritual health and spiritual growth likely for our people?

- Have they ever acted as a barrier to health and growth?

- Do our values inform how we train people and then send them out into the mission field?

- Is there ample evidence that our church holds these values as sacred?

- Could you tell by looking at us?

- Are we consistent?

- Are there areas of our lives together that aren't really shaped by our values?

If success in church planting looks like "faithfulness to what God has asked me to do" then church planters need to have some way of evaluating themselves according to that standard. The goals here are clarity in how to understand what God has asked and honesty about how faithful the planter is being. Planters can begin to measure their faithfulness in two ways: the first is to establish that they are doing the things they said they were supposed to be doing; and the second is establishing that they are leading their church to be the kind of church that God has called it to be. Churches that take self-evaluation seriously do better than churches that don't.

8

Know Your People

*Planters and plants that were prepared to adapt to the people
who actually joined them did better than those that couldn't
adjust or that longed to work with people who weren't joining
them.*

---

*"When you're starting a church you have to take
whoever comes in the door. I don't think that people
are ready for that. What happens when crazy people
come in the door? Or worse yet when someone who
rubs you the wrong way comes in?"*

Ministry among any people group requires delicacy and
courage. Since the gospel is never culturally neutral it
needs careful application. There will inevitably be
points of opposition and conflict between the host culture's value
system and those of a kingdom-shaped community. There will
also be points of congruence and similarity. These are prime
bridge-building spots where kingdom-shaped communities can
connect with their host culture's value system. Knowing when to
resist and when to lean in takes reflection and practice.

Many of the church plants in this project were
significantly engaged with a particular slice of Canadian life: the
nones. Others were exceptionally gifted with the sons and
daughters of Canadian evangelicalism: the dones. While being
connected to a specific group within Canadian culture wasn't the

case for all of the churches in our study, it was a common enough phenomenon to warrant further examination. Church plants that were able to adapt to the specific realities of the people that joined them did better than those that were unable or unwilling to do so.

Starting Points

The first reality that church plants need to take into account when serving a specific people group is the unique starting point of that people group. Churches are forced to rethink many aspects of their life together based on who shows up. For instance, a handful of churches in the study dealt with people groups that had very low education levels. Low education levels meant that literacy couldn't be assumed and certain kinds of critical reasoning processes needed to be adjusted. This can change everything from how you approach the Bible to the role of written identity statements.

Some of the churches in the study were engaged with the young adult sons and daughters of the evangelical church. To boot, many of the planters themselves fit into this category. In these cases, levels of education and literacy were not often major concerns. Instead the starting point was to consider the previous church experiences of those who showed up. Many dones come to church plants wounded. These wounds often involve "allergies" to church leadership, church structures, and practices of worship. Here is how one planter described this group:

"We had a lot of people who, when they joined us, were looking for something different. They were questioning everything and they just wanted a safe place to leave."

Note that he said a safe place to "leave," not a safe place to "live"— meaning that many among his congregation were in the process of leaving the church. That is quite a challenging starting point!

Dealing with people with severe church allergies requires a significant amount of sensitivity. Certain words, certain Christian practices, even certain forms of leadership or group decision-making can set people off. Sustained engagement also requires courage. It takes courage to compel people to move beyond their wounded state. Allergies, after all, are a debilitating problem, not a positive spiritual characteristic. Creating an allergy-free zone should only be a temporary measure. Pathological aversions to *all* forms of church leadership, *all* forms of church structure, and *all* practices of worship can be harmful to your church's ongoing health. Churches must develop their imagination for spiritual health beyond the E.R.

Some planters who had firsthand experience with their own woundedness sometimes found themselves surprised at what engaging with young evangelicals would mean. Here's how one planter put it:

> *"Many of them had a Christian memory, but I was shocked at how few of them knew how any of that applied to their actual lives. So the vision I had was just how to re-teach the Bible. It was almost as if the Bible was something they knew about, but not that it applied to them."*

Re-teaching the Bible, deepening essential understandings of the faith, and engaging in basic discipleship often comes with the dones package. They can be resistant or fearful that you are leading them back to their old kind of church. Some planters found that fear and resistance were often more pronounced among the dones than the nones.

It is worth noting that not everyone who grew up in the church was allergic to it. Some felt fine with their experience. They often wondered what all the fuss was about. However, according to the study, this has the potential to create other unique kinds of tensions within a plant. It can make collective decision-making and a sense of shared experience much more difficult. Here's how one planter described it:

> *"Basically, there were three types of people. There were people who were hardcore Christians, there were people*

> *who were on their way out of Christianity, and there were people with no religious background."*

This kind of mixture can create interesting challenges. People with no religious background are often confused by impassioned debates over tribal nuances such as music, sermons, church membership, baptism, etc.... It can be alienating and confusing to sense that certain people in your church are having an argument with their forebears—people who aren't even in the room.

In some cases, planters set out to work with a specific group of people and yet found themselves engaging with another:

> *"I went into it wanting to connect with not-yet-Christian, 18-35 year olds. What happened is that we connected with disaffected Christians who were 18-35 year olds. They felt alienated from the forms of church they had grown up and come to faith in. We had a lot of pastor's kids and missionary kids. So it was kind of a surprise."*

This kind of surprise can be disorienting. The key to adaptation for a church plant seems to be in an ability to maintain curiosity about the people who actually show up. Curiosity is the first step in understanding how to help. As has already been discussed, it is important to begin bringing to the surface the reasons for which people are joining your church. Some of those reasons will be a helpful confirmation of your values, and others will help you uncover hidden expectations and potentially problematic motivations. Learn to create healthy dialogue around these issues. Always be learning. Always be reflective. Here is some good advice:

> *"I think another factor is that when someone is in a setting that is influenced by context and culture and not learning— learning from what you see, learning from your peers, learning how the world is changing—you lose. You can't not be learning. By learning you have to find way to be in dialogue."*

Creating healthy dialogue helps make negotiating all the needs present in a church plant possible. However, negotiating can often feel risky. The needs of some can threaten the identity of others. If the planter finds themselves negotiating from a place of desperation (e.g., feeling compelled to please a particular group in order to entice them to stay), the whole conversation can feel incredibly dangerous. But that is why they pay you the big bucks... right? Here is how one planter described their desperation:

> *"Another factor was the types of people that I attracted. In my desperation, I allowed some people into the process that weren't good, and some of the people that were good I kept them at arm's length."*

Church plants need to be equal parts flexible and firm. They need to be flexible as they learn to navigate meeting the needs of people who can turn on a dime. They also need to be flexible as cherished ways of doing things will need to be up for grabs. They also need to be firm so as not to allow the broken views of the injured to dominate the conversation and direction of the church.

Life Trajectory

A second reality that church plants among specific people groups have to take into account is their group's unique life trajectory. To take an example from the study, for church plants that engaged with addicts, there was a unique sense of needing to redefine success. The direction in which an addict goes is quite different than that of a middle class, college-educated young person.

Churches that engaged with the young sons and daughters of the evangelical church needed to make significant adjustments to their lives together to account for life trajectory. For instance, young people in university are about to embark on several major life shifts. Life shifts like starting a career, getting married, and having children are important things to keep in mind for a church serving this age group. Any or all of these life shifts can affect whether people stay in the city, let alone the church plant, for the long term. This stage of life can also really affect a people group's spiritual outlook:

> *"We were helping students engage in their faith at a unique time in their own lives, when they were leaving home, rethinking their own faith and wondering if Jesus was someone they were going to commit to now that they had left their parents."*

In short, what planters told me was that church plants serving young people need to get ready for them to move away. Here's how one planter framed it:

> *"When you foster a community that is teaching people to be flexible in their spirituality, their faith journey, and their spiritual growth—the people who are drawn to that—they become more flexible in their approach to the rest of life."*

Another planter told me this:

> *"In an urban setting you have people for a maximum of six years. You see couples come to Christ, make a commitment to marriage and then begin having kids. Then they ask, 'Where are we going to live? In an urban setting?' The urban setting is more set up for singles and couples without children. We've had to put that rhythm into how we're doing church."*

Limited time horizons mean that you will need to prioritize what you do. You have to stick to the majors and adjust your thinking about how far you actually expect to get. It also means that part of your planning will need to include helping prepare people to leave well. When they go to their next city what should they be looking for? Should they work toward planting a church themselves?

Church planters need to know their people. Many of the church plants in this project were significantly engaged with the nones and the dones. These are distinctive cultures within the Canadian context and require thoughtful and sensitive work.

Engagement requires knowing when to resist and when to lean in. This takes prayerful reflection and practice. Pioneer planters need to carefully look at the starting points of their people. For nones and dones this can involve dealing with wounds created by past church experiences. Creating healthy dialogue helps make negotiating these needs possible. Pioneer planters will need to be both sensitive and firm. They will need to be sensitive by adjusting to the needs and sensitivities of nones and dones. They will need to be firm so as not to allow the broken views of the injured to solely dominate the conversation and direction of the church. Planters will also need to plan for and adapt to the unique life trajectory of their people. If they are dealing with nones and dones then life shifts like starting a career, getting married, and having children will have to be kept in mind. Planters and plants that were prepared to adapt to the people who actually joined them did better than those that couldn't adjust or that longed to work with people who weren't joining them.

9

Always Expect the Unexpected

Planters and plants that persevered through unexpected events did better than those that were unable or unwilling to keep going.

> *"I'm not a super gifted individual. I think the thing that I offer when it comes to church leadership and church planting is tenacity. And tenacity is only helpful if you stay long enough for it to kick in."*

Tenacity is an important key to sustained church planting efforts. Planting isn't always about talent and gifting. There are going to be periods when talent and gifting aren't going to get you any traction. There will be times where the only thing you will have to depend on will be your will to keep going. Tenacity will be, at times, your key to survival. That being said, it's always better to pair tenacity with a certain level of preparation. That's what this chapter is about: preparation. More accurately it's about expecting the unexpected.

In this study, most of the church plants faced "unexpected" life events. Some powered through these events, and some didn't. What I found so interesting about these "unexpected" life events was that some of them were, well, to be expected. Not everything that catches church plants off guard is a completely unexpected, meteor-from-the-heavens kind of random. There are patterns. There are things you can anticipate. There are things you can prepare for. I've collected a list in this chapter of things that commonly happen in the life of a church plant and yet often manage to catch plants off guard. If your plant anticipates and prepares for some of these possibilities, it will go a long way toward bolstering your tenacity.

Change of Venue/Location

If your church plant decides that meeting in a public space is important, beware: church plants move a lot—it comes with the territory. There are several reasons for this. One of the most common derives from the fact that church plants can't afford to pay high prices for rent. They are often forced to look for space in cheaper parts of town. Properties that are cheap to rent are often not something a landowner wants to hang on to for long, so landlords sell these properties, often. Another common reason church plants move is because they are renting from another church, and the agreement changes for some reason or another. The host church often agrees initially to the arrangement less from a magnanimous sense of joint mission and more because they need the money. It should then come as no surprise to church plants that these arrangements are subject to change. Host churches with chronic financial problems are often also unhealthy in a whole host of other ways. Because of this, they are at a great risk of closing and selling the building. Church plants beware! There is a good chance that the host church will close well before an average church plant can secure a bank loan for several million dollars. Believe it or not, that's what church buildings cost in most urban Canadian centres—and often it's more, a lot more. If the host church is fortunate enough to bounce back from their dry spell, as some of them do, then the healthier they get, the more time and space they will require. Unhealthy host churches can force a church plant to move just as easily as a healthy host can. Here's something to think about: a church plant should expect to move at least three or more times before it will land a permanent location.

For something that is so common in the life of a plant, one would think that plants would generally be better prepared for this. But the fact is that plants often aren't prepared to move. As a planter, do yourself a favour, and don't underestimate the impact of a move. Moving can change who you are and what you do. Space shapes what is possible. It can privilege certain congregational needs and ignore others. For instance, spaces that make for a cool worship environment for adults may not be as ideal for kids. Bars, cafés, and breweries are cool meeting spaces for young adults, but kids? Not so much. Space can also affect who can access life among your community. If your plant is forced to change neighbourhoods, this can affect who can be a part of your community. Access to bus routes, parking, neighbourhood demographics, and a host of other contextual factors can radically change the kinds of people that you engage with. This will in turn dramatically adjust how you live your lives together. One church planter felt as though they had planted a new church three or four times because they moved so much. Every time their meeting space changed, their neighbourhood base changed, and that meant that the kinds of people they engaged with also changed. Finally, changing space can create uncertainty. Church plants are often not ready for this:

"I think the venue conversation caused us to lose emotional steam around the vision. Our people, because they are very transient, needed consistency."

It takes actual time and energy to move—time and energy that won't be able to be devoted to deepening local leaders, collectively re-evaluating your vision, or the 101 other things that you could and should be investing in. Moving will always cost a church plant a portion of its available momentum and energy, even if done successfully.

It is important that churches plan for and talk openly about what they will do, not if, but when they move. Structure and conversations will often be a plant's only saving grace when faced with a move. Invest in these structures early as a planter—you may be surprised how soon you'll need them.

Unexpected Illness

People get sick, sometimes really sick. Unexpected illness can play a significant role in the ongoing survival of a church plant. It can be especially difficult if a key leader gets ill. In one church plant I was a part of, the planter became deathly ill one month into the launch phase. This was not a case of the sniffles. His illness meant hospitalization, surgery, and months of recovery. As God would have it, this experience did a lot of good for the church. We all had to band together. We had to bring our cares and concerns to God. We regularly engaged in prayer, and it stretched our faith. It deepened our identity and sense of community. God is good like that. But that isn't to say there were no negative consequences. First off, it was really scary. There were moments when we weren't sure if we would be able to continue. There was also a sense of lost momentum—at least a year's worth. The plant has fully recovered now, but in those early days, sickness took its toll.

Plants need to develop some contingency plans around illness. Simple things like knowing what your denomination's policies are around medical leaves can be a big help. Your denomination may also have some additional resources that you are not aware of. Check and see. Better to know and not need them than to need help and not know where to find it.

Marriage Trouble or Erosion of Spousal Support

While this one, at face value, would appear to be avoidable, it still happens—more than I care to say. At the best of times planters can struggle with a work/life balance. Not surprisingly, getting this wrong can be toxic to your primary relationships even if those relationships are strong. If you have a reluctant or even unwilling spouse then you are in trouble from the get-go. Married planters that do not approach their calling to church planting as partners are destined for disaster. Here is a free piece of advice: you should not proceed with planting if your spouse doesn't feel called as well. If they treat this as "your thing" or as just another job, you're both in trouble even before you start. Take this planter's word for it:

> *"Just know that it's not an easy thing. It's going to be hard. You've got to be willing to accept that it could be harder for some people than they can handle. For example, my wife—it was too hard for her."*

Planting isn't just another job. In the early days it will be all-consuming. It will make significant demands on your spouse and your family. If they aren't willing or able to bear up under those demands, you should *not* proceed. Sadly, in many cases the trouble does not become evident until a year or two into the plant. These kinds of problems tend to be slow emergencies. But by Year 3 or 4, whatever problems have been growing under the surface will make themselves known. It won't be pretty. Your marriage may not survive. Your ministry may not survive. The church plant may not survive. So do us all a favour and pay attention before you start.

As a couple you may need to help to uncover and overcome the demands of church planting. Check with your denomination to see if they have counselling resources available. Counselling can be an effective way to make sure you're on the same page. Counselling isn't just for couples in crisis. In fact, it can often be even more effective when there isn't a crisis. Often an outside voice can help you surface potential issues before they become a full-blown crisis. If you don't have access to a counsellor, consider speaking with another couple that has planted before. They may be able to help you find your way. Failing that, seek out the help of another mature Christian couple. Whatever you do, don't leave these issues unaddressed!

Changes in Family Circumstances

This is a broad category but an important one. It includes all kinds of changes—some happy, some sad—things like a death in the family, the birth of a child, the birth of a child with special needs, a change in your family's needs like inadequate access to schools in your neighbourhood or insufficient room in your house and the inability to afford anything larger in the neighbourhood you're planting in. All of these can affect the long-term prospects of your church planting project.

Planting affects the whole family. It is important that you are not only united as a couple but also as a family. You may not be able to do anything about all the potential challenges that come at you, but there are some things you can do before they occur. One common mistake is to not think ahead. Many church planters begin as a childless couple. Do you have a plan for how the church plant will change when you or the people in your church start having babies? Depending on the average age of the people your congregation, kids may not show up for several years. But mark my words, they will. And when they do they will tear through your childless, urban, hipster lifestyles like a knife through butter. It is best to start thinking now about developing structures and ways of life that privilege the needs of people of all ages. If you want to do this plant thing long term, you need to be willing to adapt and change once children start to come.

These are just a few of the common ways that the unexpected can directly impact your church plant. There is often very little you can do to prevent unexpected life circumstances from negatively impacting your church. They simply land in the middle of your plans and you have to deal. But that doesn't mean everything is beyond your control. Ephesians promises that God gives His church the gifts and people that they need. God's people often reveal themselves in times of emergency. It is up to us as leaders to recognize, nurture, and grow these gifts and these people. They will do much to increase your church's chances of survival.

General Preparedness

Lots of these unexpected possibilities aren't any fun to talk about. However they are even worse to live through if you are unprepared. It is important that your church get over its squeamishness and learn to talk about its general level of preparedness. The basic tool for cultivating your general preparedness, as with many things church planting-related, begins with group dialogue. A simple way to prime the pump is to play what I like to call the "Who knows?" game. As in, who knows where the keys to the space are? Who knows where the money is deposited and where the financial statements are? Who knows the denominational contact person we call if we're ever in trouble? Who knows how we would make decisions as a group if one or more of our main leaders were stuck down a mine shaft for two months? Next, it's important to collectively ask what assumptions your lives together are based on. Do we privilege a certain lifestyle or life stage? Are there too many decision-making pieces in the control of one or just a handful of leaders? Next, you could run a few of the scenarios above and ask the group how prepared they would feel if one of them happened. Finally, you could turn their attention to the future. You could ask, what kinds of processes will we need to agree to now that might help us in the future? What will this look like if things get intense or personal? Do we have an agreed-to plan for conflict resolution? Are we aware of any resources or people that could help us?

Investment in these kinds of processes might seem a little silly at first, but you will be extremely thankful that you had these conversations if something unexpected occurs.

Your Relationship with Your Denomination

Denominations can be a survival asset. In some of the stories from the study, denominations played a very helpful role when things went sideways. Denominations were often able to lend time, mediation and conflict resolution skills, helpful advice, administrative help, and support of all kinds. In some cases, they were able to send interim leaders to help a church plant through a crisis. Oftentimes, church plants are unaware of the kinds of things their denomination makes available to them should they ever need help. It can be a helpful group exercise to measure your collective awareness of the kinds of resources your denomination has to offer.

Your Personal and Collective Determination

Personal and collective determination can often be a key deciding factor in whether or not a church plant continues in the face of a crisis. This is an asset that takes time and patience to develop. I noted in the stories shared with me that sometimes the only thing that kept a church going was their collective will to keep it going. Here is how one planter described what happened when he decided to quit and the church wanted to keep going:

> *"People were hurt because if I had stuck it out we could have kept going. Even though I had all those issues, they said, we could have kept going."*

The decision to continue is always two-sided: the planter and the church both get a say. The happy news, in this particular case, is that no less than two churches began from the ashes of this church plant. Better still, they both continue today. Never underestimate the power of simply deciding to keep on keeping on.

You can cultivate this asset by frequently and collectively revisiting your reasons for being a church in the first place. As I have mentioned already, unmet expectations and the erosion of hope are two of the biggest church plant killers. These can only be combatted when your reasons for continuing are more compelling than your reasons for quitting. Is your reason for existence being there for one another? Then regularly reminding yourselves of that can help you survive just about anything. Are you called to a specific neighbourhood? Then regularly reminding yourselves of that can help you survive just about anything. In the words of one planter:

"The biggest difference between success and failure, I can only attribute it to perseverance. The parachute mentality doesn't work. It's churches who take up residence that succeed."

As a church, your collective ability to hear from and respond to God is vital. Regularly engage with God. Ask Him to help you, as a church, to develop the spiritual gift of perseverance. Learn to listen to the heart of God. Spend time asking Him to help purify the reasons your church exists in the first place. As a group, discuss ways that you could collectively develop the spiritual gift of perseverance. Listen to what this planter had to say:

"Perseverance actually is a spiritual gift. I have literally done hundreds of things where I wasn't sure if even one person would come. Whether we kept going could not be based on that. Church planting is so slow. We did what we did because God asked us to do it. We're going to keep going until God tells us to do something different. If we had based our work on anything else we never would have survived. Progress is just too slow."

Perseverance is a gift from God and an asset you can develop. Pray you won't need to put it to the test. However if you do, having perseverance will grant you the resources you need to survive.

Church plants should expect that one or more of the above things will happen to them in the normal course of their life together. Churches that actively invest in perseverance do better than those that simply react to whatever comes their way. You can invest in survival assets, but you must do it while the waters are smooth—in the middle of the storm it is often too late. As a leader it is important that you develop a safe and helpful way to discuss the unexpected with your congregation. You can start by regularly assessing and developing your general level of preparedness. This can be as simple as making sure people know what to do in a handful of possible situations. Next, acquaint yourselves with the resources that your denomination makes available. These can be lifesavers should you ever need them. Finally, you'll want to turn your attention to your collective determination. Collective determination comes from your reasons for being a church in the first place. Regularly inviting your group to talk about why you are a church will help clarify and deepen these reasons. Finally, and most importantly, learn how to submit to God's will. Ask Him to lead and guide you. Ask Him what purposes He has for your church. Ask Him to give you the gift of perseverance.

10

Take a LITTLE Help from Your Friends

 Plants that received occasional or modest help from outside sources did better than those that depended heavily on outside sources for survival.

"Stop giving church planters so much money!"

This was perhaps one of the most counter-intuitive insights I uncovered from the whole study. Common wisdom would suggest that the more financial support a church plant can get their hands on the better, but this is simply not the case. Just as overwatering a flower can increase its chances of developing root rot, so too an overabundance of external support can impede the normal development of a church plant. This can happen in several ways.

Unstable Budgeting

Church plants that received an overabundance of financial support from external sources were very vulnerable to fluctuations in budgeting. In an alarming number of cases the church plant was utterly dependent on external funding sources to sustain its operating budget. This sounds good in theory, but in practice it can be a nightmare. It is not uncommon for external organizations and donors to fall on hard times. Hard times for others can create an acute financial crisis for you as a church plant. This problem was so severe for some plants in the study that they suggested it would have been better to get nothing, or at least way less money, than to ride a financial roller coaster. One year they were flush with cash, and the next there was nearly nothing. This made budgeting exceedingly difficult and proved demoralizing for both the church and the planter. Pay attention. Bouncing paycheques can also erode your family's capacity to hang in there!

Even in stable funding environments there can be challenges with overdependence on external support. Here is a fact that very few planters pay attention to: a denomination's funding formula normally decreases over four or five years. When you don't pay attention to this, you inevitably run into problems. Imagine that a denomination's funding formula looks like this: $40K in Year 1, $30K in Year 2, $20K in Year 3, $10K in Year 4. That seems like a pretty good formula: not too much, not too little. But pay attention! If a plant doesn't think ahead, they could find themselves chronically underfunded by $10K annually for the first four years of their existence. Let me break it down for you. If you had this funding model, your plant would have to find an additional $10K every year just to maintain its budget. In the first few years of existence an extra $10K can be difficult to come up with on a consistent basis. Trouble would deepen if your church is like most churches, and your budget grows over time. Costs always go up. The need and desire to expand is natural and important. However, if you add growth pressure to a chronic shortfall you have a recipe for financial difficulty.

Be aware of your denomination's funding model. Be aware of its implications. Share that awareness with the people in your church. Find ways to help them to practically understand the burden. In the scenario described above, one way forward would be to take the $10K amount and divide it by the number of people who are a part of the church. For instance, if there were 20 of you, each of you would need to come up with an extra $500 per year to give in order to maintain what the church has. That's $1000 per year per couple. It should be noted that these difficulties are seldom insurmountable. Church plants survive them all the time. In fact, the financial stretching is healthy and faith-enriching—but at least be aware of it as you set your budget.

Split Focus

An overabundance of external money can also result in a split focus—just ask any missionary or Christian worker that raises their own support and they will tell you that donor maintenance can be close to a full-time job. Even if the hours don't amount to full time, the emotional investment and worry certainly can. But that isn't the only way external fundraising can interfere. External fundraising can also hinder the normal functioning of leadership.

In one case a church plant felt fortunate to have multiple people "on staff" with less than 100 people in the congregation. That size of staff would be impossible under normal circumstances and yet external fundraising made it possible. So why not, right? Unfortunately, a few years into the life of the plant, two things happened. The first was that giving did not grow to make their staffing commitments sustainable. External support was interfering with the natural tension between what the church wanted and what it could afford. The second was that external support dried up for some of the staff in the plant and not for others. Those that didn't meet the fund raising goals had to be laid off. The church simply couldn't afford them on its own steam. This new arrangement created all kinds of tension in the church and among the staff. The decision about which staff continued and which ones didn't was not based on what made sense from a leadership perspective or on the needs of the church. The decision was dictated by external funding sources. A good church planting budget is meant to reflect local needs and capacities. Theirs was completely divorced from their context.

The disconnect meant that the church was eventually unable to continue.

Unrealistic Structures

Overfunding from external sources can impede the development of realistic structures, especially structures that need to be contextually-specific. If the goal of the plant is long-term work in a specific location among a specific people group then the plant will need to develop a budget that is realistic for that context. Churches need to be aware of both their internal carrying capacity and the carrying capacity of the neighbourhood. External funding interferes with a church plant's natural sense of these factors. Overfunding can make plants vulnerable to creating oversized plans and systems that don't match their context. Here's an example of what that can look like on the ground:

> "I always accepted that this church would not be financially sustainable by its people. But while I was getting money to lead from the denomination, I started to meddle a little bit and started to add more stuff to what we were doing: more groups, more events, more stuff. It would have been better if I had just left things alone and let it grow slowly—or waited until someone else came along and added something. I didn't give it enough time to catch on."

Financial sustainability is a relative term. All contexts can be financially sustainable if your budget is zero. You can run on that forever. However, zero money budgets are rare—I personally haven't seen one. Even church plants in the developing world require money to operate. Developing a context-sensitive budget requires that you listen to and feel out your neighbourhood. Too little money can choke out your development and rob you of opportunities. It can also mean you risk not developing a culture of generosity and financial stewardship among your people. This has very serious discipleship consequences. Lack of financial stewardship is a particularly acute problem for Canadians. At the time of writing, Canadians are among the worst savers in the developed world. Church plants that do not address this problem are overlooking one of the largest discipleship issues of our time. Lack of generosity is toxic to spiritual health. One planter made this suggestion to external donors:

> *"Give just enough to make it safe to step off the cliff but not so much that we don't have to exercise real stewardship ourselves."*

There is no magic ratio for giving that suits all circumstances. You must do this by feel. Such decisions must be made between the denomination and the plant and on a case-by-case basis.

Realistic budgets are necessarily a local matter, and must be worked out over time. The more dependent you become on outside inputs, the slower your local development will be. In the end it might be best to be conservative in your planning and amend as you go rather than promising much and delivering little. Stability is always the key. Without it I have watched church plants needlessly erode the planter family's ability to stay at it long term. An unrealistic or unsustainable church budget quickly becomes an unrealistic or unsustainable family budget. This can be very demoralizing. To be frank, it can feel as though the church doesn't appreciate the planter's efforts and sacrifices. This kind of behaviour is utterly corrosive and can lead directly to the end of the church plant.

Lack of Contextual Creativity

Overfunding can impede the proper development of contextual creativity of a church plant as it removes some of the pressure to be realistic. Without such pressure, a plant won't be as likely to actively seek out novel solutions that work in their context. Pressure to make this plant sustainable—here, in this place—is irreplaceable fuel for your church's imagination. It's a gift that no one wants, but at the same time it can be totally indispensable. Here's what one planter had to say:

> *"On an organizational level you can't expect that your church is going to grow enough numerically to support you*

financially, which is what most church models are built around organizationally. So you'll have to think about other ways of doing [church]. Especially, if you're dealing with a poor community—the more that people come, the bigger your financial need is going to be. So you have to think about another way of doing things there."

One of the gifts of planting is an opportunity to explore new ways of being the church. Too much external financial support makes us less likely to explore.

Lack of Group Ownership

External overfunding can impede the proper development of group ownership within a church plant. The will to survive properly resides within the plant itself, and must be built piece by piece from a deep sense of God's calling and a deep burden for the needs of the neighbourhood. Too much outside support can make someone else the owner and can cause a church plant to take on someone else's expectations. Ideally, you want to keep your church plant's reasons for being as clean as possible. You want to keep your church plant free from any expectation other than creating an environment where people from your specific context can meet Jesus and have their lives transformed. Prioritizing any other expectation complicates and ultimately damages the church.

Lack of Local Leaders

Dependence on external funding isn't the only way outsiders can impede the natural development of a church plant. Dependence on external leadership can also stunt a plant's growth. Some churches from the study began with a leadership group that was made up of people who were not actually a part of the plant. This made sense in the early days, but it became a serious problem. Some of these plants are only now, after 7 to 10 years existence, starting to develop local leaders. This is way too long to wait. If you insist on external leadership as part of your strategy, it is important to keep this state of affairs as short as possible—a year or two at the most. However, an even better alternative might be to allow yourself more time to develop your core group before the plant begins rather than to seed the leadership pool with people from the outside. Anything that robs you as a planter of a sense of urgency to develop local leaders should be seen as extremely problematic and avoided whenever possible.

So what are some the things that you can do to avoid the negative effects of external inputs? I am certainly not saying that church plants should be left to fend for themselves entirely—quite the opposite, in fact. Denominations and other groups can play a vital role in helping get church plants off the ground. However, the key is for the denomination or networks to avoid excessive amounts of helping. To avoid overhelping, denominations and networks should occasionally review their funding models and strategies with church plants to ensure that what they are doing still works. Planters would also do well to check their own motivations for church planting. What if you could never earn a salary from a church plant? Would you still do it? If not, then church planting might not be for you.

We are facing an uncertain future when it comes to full-time paid clergy in Canada. If a full-time salary is your minimum standard for entering the ministry, then you may be in trouble before you begin. We also face an uncertain future for funding church plants in general. So we need to begin some earnest and honest dialogue about how we move forward. There is such a thing as too much funding. Too much funding creates all kinds of developmental problems for plants.

We've done a lot of talking about the negative effects of too much funding, but what about the downside of too little funding? I discovered two basic challenges of church plants that have too little funding. The first is that underfunded church plants are not able to afford rental spaces in most of Canada's urban cores. Do we need to afford rental spaces? Good question. That answer will have to be worked out on the ground. It will depend on context, and on the kind of church God is asking you to plant. On one hand, it's hard to seem like you're a part of the neighbourhood if you don't have bricks and mortar. Then again, constantly defaulting to using buildings might be a failure of our collective imagination. The second challenge of underfunding is whether or not it is feasible to ask a lifelong planter to voluntarily commit financial suicide every five years or so whenever they start a new church. The quick answer to that is no, it isn't. But again, the question itself might be a failure of imagination. And, again I'm happy to let planters help us answer that.

For now the risk we face is that so long as we need spaces (which we might) and so long as people need to make a living from planting (which they might), money will always be a part of this conversation. Settling what we mean when we say too much or not enough funding is what needs to be the goal of our ongoing dialogue.

11

Broaden Your Shoulders

Planters who were able to share leadership did better than plants in which the majority of energy and authority was localized in the planter.

"*Even if you have people that are extremely gifted and extremely determined to do it on their own, it's not healthy to let them do it on their own. They need the support of other like-minded people.*"

One planter called the work of deepening leadership capacity in his church "growing broader shoulders." To him, growing broader shoulders meant not only that the church was able to do more, but that the energy and authority in the church was not solely localized in him. As a result the church was able to mount more ambitious projects and deal with increasingly diverse groups of people. It also meant that the church had more ownership of the vision, but this shift came with a cost. Developing "broader shoulders" meant investing increasing amounts of time with a handful of key leaders. That meant that he as a planter wasn't spending time with everyone equally. It meant that he wasn't as engaged on the frontlines. It may not sound all that revolutionary on the surface but it was significant departure from the way he led in the early days of the plant. For some planters, this kind of shift can be very threatening identity-wise. But for those who can make these adjustments peacefully, it can mean the difference between continuing and not continuing as a plant. This church plant's story was far from unique; it was paralleled in several other churches in the study. Others noticed that they needed to make shifts to develop a broader base of leaders in their plant as well, and some were more successful than others.

From the outset it should be noted that sharing leadership is a skill. This means that not everyone can do it well at first. It can take time to learn, and it's often not immediately rewarding. It takes consistent, methodical practice, emotional maturity, and considerable energy. The only way you will stay on this road is if you see value in what you are doing. Leadership sharing is vital, and it is possible. You'll just need to invest in some key areas.

Invest in Group Self-Understanding

I know I'm starting to sound like a broken record here, but my point in emphasizing group self-understanding bears repeating because it is so important. Sometimes planters resist investing into their plant in this way because it seems counter to life in the Spirit or doesn't feel quite organic enough. But this kind of work goes right back to the book of Acts, Acts 6 specifically. Luke tells us:

> "In those days when the number of disciples was increasing, the Hellenistic Jews among them complained against the Hebraic Jews because their widows were being overlooked in the daily distribution of food" (Acts 6:1).

Was it true that there were ethnic reasons for some of the church members getting fed while others remained in need? Given the deep-seated ethnocentricity of the pre-persecuted early church, one would not be surprised if this was partially true. However, I can't help but wonder if this dilemma was also partially caused by the apostles being overloaded with newly-emerging logistical challenges.

Imagine for a second that you belong to a group of 12 people who are responsible for the spiritual well-being of thousands upon thousands of people. You started as a leader of a group of about 120 people, and now there might be as many as 25,000 people. Of those folks you can count on as many as 800 to 1,000 widows per day in need of something to eat. From a purely logistical standpoint, feeding that many people is no easy task. How would you manage the intake of widows in need? How would you know who they were and what they needed? How would you organize your food supply? Potlucks for 10 are simple. But add another 990 people and you're dealing with something entirely different. So what did this group of twelve do about it? They called people together to talk. They talked about who they were as a community. At that point, their self-understanding was that they, as a community, had at least two vitally important jobs to do. The first was the ministry of prayer and the preaching of the word of God. The second was waiting on tables. These were the two identity pieces that they realized about themselves. So they organized the church around those two core functions. Notice the transition there. Before this meeting their collective self-understanding had not been articulated. It was real but no one had bothered to put it in words. Now, after the meeting, they knew that these two things were central to who they were. As we continue to read, we see that this plan made the Spirit and the group happy and so they chose other leaders to help them live into this new reality. Luke tells us that explosive growth resulted:

"So the word of God spread. The number of disciples in Jerusalem increased rapidly, and a large number of priests became obedient to the faith" (Acts 6:7).

The church now had broader shoulders. They were capable of more. More people were able to depend on them. Sometimes organizing can be a deeply spiritual exercise. It can be a profound act of obedience and faithfulness. It involves asking who you are and what you should be putting your energy into. Churches that take this kind of work seriously do better than those who don't.

Invest in a Small Group of Leaders

Before we leave the story of Acts we should also note the group's investment into a small group of leaders. Even though the group identified its core functions as the ministry of prayer and the word and the ministry of waiting on tables that didn't mean that everyone in the church divided the jobs amongst themselves and went to work. They set aside leaders to accomplish this. It wasn't a particularly massive group either: they set aside seven people. I saw a similar phenomenon happen among the church plants in the study. Here's where that shift started for one planter. He noted that:

> *"We had no shortage of ministry but a definite shortage of ministers. And yet there was all the evidence in the world that we were needed in this neighbourhood."*

This is a helpful way to look at need in your church: need is never in short supply. You can find it anywhere and everywhere. If you want to do something effective about the needs around you for the long term, you'll need other leaders who can help. Developing leaders takes time, energy, and focus. To do this will mean pulling yourself away from the frontlines and investing in a few leaders. Planters that don't feel guilty every time they focus on their inner circle of leaders do better than those who resist this kind of investment.

Here are some questions to help you start focusing on investing in leaders. First and foremost you need to start getting specific. You need to ask:

- Who do we have in our congregation?
- Do I have a handful of people in mind?
- Can I name names?
- Next, are these names a regular part of my calendar?

As you continue to develop collective self-understanding you can begin to ask:

- Can the leaders I work with link what they do to what the church is about?
- Can I double up my efforts?
- Should I spread that around?

Finally, as a leadership group, you can begin to set goals together. You need to continue to act and think as a body. Listen to the hard-won wisdom of one planter:

> *"I think some of the folly, some of the slowness, some of the tiredness we experienced is because there wasn't a full blown body of Christ... being the body of Christ."*

This work is collective; it requires frequently revisiting your self-understanding as a church. Things change. The early church experienced change too. They didn't stay as a group with two core functions for long. Change began almost immediately. Shortly after being chosen, Stephen, one of the seven table servers was arrested and stoned to death. Persecution broke out against the church and the church was scattered and went underground. Almost overnight they went from a Jerusalem-based entity to one that spread through the empire. As they spread they became less and less exclusively Jewish, less and less exclusively centred around life in Jerusalem, and less and less exclusively under the control of Peter and the other apostles. New kinds of leaders began to emerge. All of these radical shifts required the apostles, as a leadership community, to wrestle with their new reality. They had to keep asking, who are we now? The answer required listening to the Spirit. It required responding to the people that were coming. It required wisdom and reasonable, measured responses. It required empowering leaders to explore new directions and ministries. It required council meetings and leadership decisions. Church plants need to be able to do the same.

Invest in Learning Moments

The pressure to always be the person who knows what to do can be very real for a planter. In the early years, church planters are always making decisions on their own and are often needed to be the final authority on important matters. As the months and years roll by, this pattern becomes well established and can be tough to disrupt. The group gets used to it. Add the fact that autocratic leadership is often super-efficient to the mix, and you have the perfect conditions for delaying the development of body-based decision-making. Church planters and their churches have to unlearn these bad habits if they are to mature and expand. That's why it is important to watch yourself and your leadership as a planter during periods of uncertainty. These "learning moments" can be important opportunities to learn how to live together in a new way. Here are a couple of practical suggestions for how you might go about doing that.

The first trick is to learn to be quieter in meetings. Do you notice all the eyes on you when it comes time to come up with an answer? Take a risk and allow for some awkward silences. Use this moment to ask if anyone else has an idea. Some leaders find this threatening, but it is a key to unleashing the body.

Another trick is to learn the power of three words: "I don't know." This can be incredibly hard for some leaders to say. And yet, saying "I don't know" can create a valuable space in which other leaders can grow and new ideas can emerge. Even if you do have an idea or two, learning how to hold them back and let the group wrestle with problems can be transformative for both you and them. If you rush the group from problem to solution, you stunt the development of leadership capacity. Take your time. Spend more time developing the group's understanding of the problem. Slow things down and pray. Allow quieter or more hesitant voices to speak. Squeeze all you can out of these moments.

Invest in Other Networks

Another key strategy in growing broader shoulders is to begin investing in networks. Planters who did this well invested in two basic directions.

The first direction is toward networks where you rub shoulders with people who are similar to you. One planter put it this way:

"From the very beginning I had this thought: if you're doing anything like me then we've got to get together once a month; it's essential. There were times when we really had to cry on each other's shoulders. Church planting, especially out-of-the-box church planting like we were doing, is very lonely. I didn't feel like I could talk to too many people about it."

Connecting with others is an investment. It takes time, attention, and sometimes even money. But it can be key to developing your skills as a leader. People who are facing many of the same challenges as you can offer unique insights into your situation. Here's what one participant told me about the value of networks of similar people:

"There is a lot of momentum gained in those circles. You get to test some of your ideas against people who are actually doing it. You don't have to feel like you're crazy because you're trying to do something new."

There is a lot to be gained in finding people who "get it." It can ease your loneliness, it can give you support, and it can allow you to find understanding about where you're coming from at the deepest level.

Planters also invested well by investing in a network of people who were dissimilar to them. Not all problems encountered by church plants are unique. People are still people. Pastors in established churches can be a wealth of knowledge and wisdom. But don't limit yourself to just the church. Planters who invested in networks well engaged with people who did all kinds of things. Talk to people in the not-for-profit sector, people who manage volunteers, people who work in creative fields, and people who work as entrepreneurs. Basically, anyone who deals with managing people for a living can provide you with insights. One planter said this about working with people different than himself:

"I need other people. Given the amount of understanding, the careful discussions, and the need for proper communication that is needed to have a vision become reality, to have dreams to become solid, to have a solid harmonized plan, I need other people to help me."

Developing leaders isn't something that only church plants struggle with. Established churches and organizations of all kinds have learned valuable lessons in doing this kind of work. You can learn a lot from them.

Growing broader shoulders is a skill, meaning that not everyone will be able to do it well at first. You'll need to begin by investing in collective self-understanding. This will help your church clarify what it needs to be doing and provide insight into who you'll need to help. Next you'll need to invest in a small group of leaders. Planters often avoid doing this because they feel guilty when they pull focus from the frontlines in order to be with a smaller group of people, but investing in your leaders is vital. Thirdly, you'll need to learn to invest in "learning moments." By learning not to rush people to find solutions, you can create space for leadership and new ideas to grow. Finally, you'll need to invest in networks. Church planters who did this well learned to take advantage of networks of people who were like them and networks of people who were not like them. The diversity of those two perspectives helped them to fill in the gaps of their own leadership and find new ways to lead.

12

Keep 'Em Separated

Plants that did not tie their survival to a business did better than those that did tie their plant to a business.

"The necessity of running the day-to-day operations to fund the ministry became so all-consuming so fast."

An idea I hear frequently in the church planting world is one where the worlds of business and church are joined together. Usually the idea is to open a church in a café. The logic is that by drawing on the strengths of both of these worlds, both the church and the business can be stronger. This works well on paper but seldom in practice. Here are some practical reasons why this isn't the wisest course of action.

Of the handful of church plants in the study that tied a business to their church, a full 75% of them are no longer continuing. This fact alone should give one pause. The few plants that did survive this kind of arrangement did one key thing: they did not tie the survival of the business and the survival of the church together. They kept 'em separate. There are several reasons why this is a good idea. Let's look at a few of them together.

Church plants have a higher survival rate on their own

First and perhaps foremost, there really is no compelling reason to tie the survival of a business and the survival of a church together. The fact is that church plants have a higher survival rate than businesses do. Here's what I mean: the pioneer church plants in our study only experienced a 48% closure rate after 10 years. Compare that fact with what H.G. Parsa discovered about restaurants in the U.S.: that around 60% of American restaurants fail after the first three to five years.[14] For cafés the number is actually closer to 70%.[15] Since many of the business ideas that church plants attempt tend to be related to the food service industry, this statistic is particularly salient. Church planters that tie the survival of their church plant to a food service-based business are needlessly placing their plant at a higher risk. Here's how one planter described their meltdown:

> *"It's an interesting dynamic because you have a dual purpose—not only are you promoting the church, but you are also endeavouring to build the business. So there's an interesting mind game that goes on: which master at which time am I serving? Unfortunately, the master that needed $20,000 dollars a month was often the one that got first priority."*

It's impossible to know how their church would have fared if it had not been tied to the business. Given the high stakes involved it's hard to see the upside of this type of an arrangement. The dangers, more often than not, outweigh the potential.

Many planters lack business acumen

Most of the planters I talked to who added a business to their planting plan did not have a business background or any previous experience in running a business before they began. If

---

[14] Parsa, 309-312.
[15] Parsa, 312.

you plan on starting a new church/business plant take heed: those who have gone on before you tell me that this should be a major red flag. Establishing and sustaining a profitable business requires genuine talent. The establishing part involves compliance with local, provincial, and federal regulatory bodies, purchasing expensive equipment to comply with health and safety standards, developing profitable deals with food distributors, navigating insurance and payroll, an understanding of tax and charitable law, and knowledge of restaurant design and menu planning–not to mention the extensive market testing that any serious business would require to determine if a profit could actually be made at that specific location. This is a science! Skilled entrepreneurs determine things like market saturation, market trends, projected demand, and countless other factors. Starbucks and Tim Hortons don't just buy any old patch of land and set up shop. Even though they have a tried and tested product and significant market share in their niche, there is a lot of work that goes into picking the right location. Very few planters I talk to who include starting a business in their planting plans are doing the market research or developing the business plans required to be successful. No one in the business world would ever dream of doing this. So, why would a church plant? Here's some final food for thought: if you want to succeed in the coffee business, you need to be better than Starbucks or Tim Hortons at some aspect of the coffee game. If you aren't better you will likely fail.

Okay so that is just the basics of what you need to do to get a business opened. The process can take years and is always exhausting and complicated. We haven't even scratched the surface on how to keep the business open and profitable. Sustainability in business involves intensive study of your business. You have to determine how to maximize profitability, streamline business functions, and correctly anticipate and adjust to changes in the industry. By 2005, a mid-90s, "Friends"-style coffee shop was no longer as profitable as it was when it first started. People's tastes and demands change—often. Do you really want to take on the need to reinvent your business every 10 years alongside all the other things you need to pay attention to in establishing and sustaining a church? The challenge for many in the study is that their business plans simply did not work. The fundamental rule of business—bring in more money than you spend—may be simple to say but it's much harder to do. Here's how one participant described it:

"We were doing the slow bleed. So, losing a $1,000 or $1,500 per month."

Losses like this aren't uncommon in business, but they can also be really difficult to diagnose and fix, even for experienced business people. A slow bleed can eventually be fatal. In many cases in our study, that slow bleed not only took out the business, but the church as well.

Planting and entrepreneurship are both all-consuming

For those that do have enough business skill to establish and sustain a business there is yet another challenge. Establishing and sustaining a business is an all-consuming project. Any business owners will tell you that running a business isn't a 9-5 job. It demands more time than that! It will eat up your whole life. Most planters described their work in establishing a church in similar terms, especially in the early days. So what makes you imagine that you can do both at the same time?

Planters that try to do both inevitably struggle with exhaustion. The toll can be greater than simply stress and tiredness; it can profoundly and negatively affect other aspects of your life as well. Here's an example of paying a higher than expected price:

"Working all week at the business and then going back on the weekend to do church just destroyed us as a couple, and the ministry folded."

Fortunately in this case the marriage did survive but recovery, even years later, remains incomplete. In some cases, the planter may be able to bounce back from a setback like this but often the spouse does not. Everyone bears the weight of this stress differently and recovery times vary. If you decide to try and tackle two life-consuming projects at the same time, you may wind up paying a higher than expected price.

Planters that try to do both at the same time also pay a price in having divided loyalties. It is difficult to give full attention to both of these very important and demanding projects. Here's what one planter said about that phenomenon:

"Probably within five or six months, the ministry started to take a back seat emotionally and physically to this monster that we created in order to begin a ministry."

By sustaining these divided loyalties over a long period of time, many planters found themselves having to choose one project over the other. Most planters, of course, start with the idea that the business will serve the church or at least get along with it in a symbiotic kind of way. But this isn't how things tend to work themselves out practically. Usually it winds up that the church is asked to serve and sacrifice for the business. Why? Because invoices for overdue rent tend to be more compelling than a vague sense that spiritual health isn't progressing as well as it should. If either or both of the projects begin to flounder, it can be hard to know which one to save first. In the words of one planter:

"When the cracks start to show you just try what you're doing harder. You just put in more effort, less sleep, and more money."

It's pretty clear how quick this can become an unsustainable way to operate. Divided loyalties may work for a time but they don't work over the long haul.

Churches and businesses exist for different reasons

A business and a church have two very different sets of assumptions, values, and reasons for existing. These fundamental differences mean they don't always cooperate with each other when you tie them together for survival. One of the things that I noticed in the study is that often, when a business should have been behaving like a business, they acted like a church. Conversely, when a church should have been acting like a church, they acted like a business. So let's look at these fundamental differences to get a sense of where things go wrong.

Fundamentally, businesses need to make a profit. That of course means they must take in more money than they spend. A profit margin is the only thing that makes a business possible. It's what enables growth, the hiring of staff, and just the general momentum of things. At the end of the day, a profit margin is what transforms something from a fun hobby into something that you do for a living. Making coffee for other people can be fun and rewarding. What moves that from a fun side project to something you do for a living is a specific dollar figure. That dollar figure has to match the annual amount of money that your family can live on. Businesses that cannot produce that dollar amount every year do not survive. It's that simple. It's your basic business score card: a healthy business has a healthy profit margin.

So what does it look like when a business starts to act like a church? This process begins when profits don't materialize. We often see this most clearly in the area of staffing. Why? Because staffing tends to be the biggest ticket item in business expenditures. In the normal world, if profits cannot pay for staff, the business cannot continue and decisions must be made. The business will be forced to either borrow money in hopes of future profitability (a high risk proposition) or to cut staff, to cut expenses, to shrink the business, or even to close the business altogether. Churches that start businesses often create another option, which is to staff the business with volunteers. At first it can seem like a good idea, because what churches lack in money they can often make up for in volunteers. However, by "solving" the problem with volunteers, the church isn't addressing the underlying fundamental health problems of the business. The business is no longer a functional business. It has, in effect, reverted back to a side project or a hobby of the church. The business becomes dependent on the church to keep sending volunteers, and if that stops, the business stops. Now let's look at this challenge from the church's perspective to see how this can go even further sideways.

Fundamentally, churches are meant to be focused on creating an environment that promotes and expects spiritual development; their existence depends on it. In other words, churches exist due to their ability to take in people from their context, introduce them to Jesus, baptize them, teach them how to be His disciples, and help them find their place in doing the same for others. Any other focus clouds the purpose of the church: a focus on growing Sunday morning worship attendance clouds the purpose of the church; a desire to prove you're not like all the other churches clouds the purpose of the church. A church's survival is entirely dependent on the spiritual development of its members. That's Job One. If a church merely recycles Christians from other churches, it will eventually cave in on itself. If a church remains so maladapted to its context that no one new joins from the context, it will shrivel and die. If a planter can't, doesn't, or won't lead their church to introduce people to Jesus, baptize them, and teach them how to be His disciples, then the church will be something other than the church. If a planter can't, doesn't, or won't lead their church to engage these disciples in mission then the church will be something other than the church. It's your basic church score card: a healthy church promotes and expects spiritual development.

So what does it look like when a church begins acting like a business? Well, subtly at first, another focus is introduced into its discipleship. If a church depends on a business to survive, then the temptation will consistently be to turn the church into a mechanism for shaping people into volunteers for the business, or its customers. This is clearly not the church. Running a business can also complicate a church's relationship with people outside the church. Are they people in need of Jesus or potential customers? One planter put the dilemma this way:

"How do you invite people to your church in such a way as to not lose their business?"

None of the churches in our study went into this kind of arrangement with the goal of confusing things. They did it because they wanted to find a meaningful way to interact with people in their context. The key mistake here is not that the business world and the church world don't have any overlap— they certainly do. They can even enjoy a healthy symbiotic relationship with each other, that is, if you keep 'em separate. At their hearts, churches and businesses exist for very different reasons. Because of this, they simply can't be arranged in such a way as to prop up and ensure the survival of the other.

So am I saying that churches and businesses can't ever be in relationship together? Is there no way that a business and a church can function side by side? Based on what I've observed, before a church planter chooses to enter into any kind of relationship with a business they will want to keep several things straight. The first, since you are approaching this new venture as a church planter, you need to stay in that role. In other words, don't stray into business entrepreneur territory. Your primary goal is to establish a community that promotes and nurtures Christian spiritual development. Anything that competes, distracts, or otherwise interferes with that purpose should be flagged immediately and avoided. Ask yourself, in what way does partnering with this business directly relate to our mission? Is the person starting this business someone other than me? Do they have a background in business? Do they have a background specifically in the business they are starting? Do we have a way of determining the missional effectiveness of this relationship? What signs have we decided on beforehand that will serve as our cue to exit the relationship? Second, be sure that you are aware of issues around survival, which is where things really tend to go sideways. Ask yourself a couple of questions: how will we survive as a church in the *likely* event that this business tanks? Does our future vision depend on increasing or decreasing our dependence on this business? Is my family implicated in the survival of this business in any way? Am I being asked to co-opt church functions and practices to serve or otherwise prop up bad business practices? If this isn't happening now, how we will detect this as a group if things change in the future? Third, since planting and starting a business are both all-consuming, you should ensure that your efforts as a planter, your salary, and your time is in no way significantly tied to the business. Fourth, make yourself aware of the potential implications for your congregation. Ask yourself: is there any pressure whatsoever on our people to be involved in propping up the business—either as a customer or as volunteer staff? Both of these are classic ways churches ignore bad business practices. Finally, are you knowledgeable about the Canadian tax laws that create serious distinctions between charitable activities and business activities? If you aren't, you should be.

In a world full of possibilities when it comes to being the church, there may be a reason for a church to develop close links with a business. However, based on the findings of this study, churches should avoid making hasty or ill-advised relationships with business owners. Failure to do so can put your church plant at an artificially-increased risk.

13

Your Denomination Matters

Planters who were connected with denominations with a high capacity for nurturing and supporting pioneer church planting did better than those whose denominations had little to no capacity for support and nurturing them.

"It's going to be a double-edged sword supporting new things. The new things are going to want to push out further from the denomination—further than a denomination is ever going to be comfortable with. If you, as a denomination, are going to embrace new forms of church you are going to be stretched and forced to come to grips with your own values and ways of doing things. You are going to be tested. The new groups are going to do things differently, in ways that makes sense to them."

You may be surprised to learn that a majority of the church plants in the study were part of a denomination. Church planters have a reputation for being independent spirits, and that tends to go double for pioneer church planters. While I think this reputation is earned in some cases, it would appear that in the majority of cases this independence is tempered: tempered by a desire to live inside a historical tradition; tempered by a somewhat amorphous desire to be "accountable to someone"; tempered by a desire to find colleagues who are different. Most planters in the study expressed an appreciation of the support of their denomination. As a general finding, I would say that denominations in Canada get a passing grade for their support of pioneer church planting. Apart from a few sad stories, this chapter has some good news for denominations. What follows should be taken in the spirit of "a job well done" but there a couple of areas where denominations can improve together. Good news aside, there were at least two stories in which a denomination played a direct and undeniable role in ending the church plant in their care. Given the relatively small sample size of our study, two is a significant number, so we'll also look into these cases in greater depth.

During the interviews I asked planters if they had any advice for denominations that want to do a good job of supporting pioneer church planting. They mentioned several factors that they felt would positively contribute to a better relationship between a pioneer planter and their denomination.

Examine Your Need for Control

The most consistent word of advice from planters surrounded a denomination's need for control. Their basic suggestion was that the higher the denomination's need for control, the worse the relational outcome. The negative control came from two basic needs: a denomination's need for wins, and a denomination's need to fully understand.

Denominational leaders with a need for "wins"— meaning church plants must always succeed—created a negative environment for pioneer church planters. It should go without saying that if you are operating in a denominational climate where you cannot afford to fail, ever, then the denomination shouldn't engage in church planting in the first place. It's common knowledge that not all church plants work out. Plants can fail even if they use paint-by-number-style models, have a properly assessed planter who is trained and coached, and have adequate funding. Pioneer church planting comes with increased risk. The good news is that most denominations understand this, but not all. Problems arise for pioneer church plants when they belong to a denomination that has a particular aversion to things not working out. Aversions to things not working out find their source in either pragmatism or theological beliefs. For instance, some denominations lack adequate financial resources. Denominations in this position are often vulnerable to pressure that they can't afford to fail. This pressure creates a pragmatic aversion to things not working out. If you are part of a denomination that falls into this category, pioneer church planting shouldn't be considered. For the sake of your denomination's planting department, and for the sake of the ministry of pioneer planters, it would be better if your denomination referred pioneer planters to work with another group.

Problems can also arise for denominations where failure carries theological weight. Verses like "no weapon formed against you will prevail" (Isaiah 54:7) and "I will build my church, and the gates of Hades will not overcome it" (Matthew 16:16) can be interpreted to mean that plans that are seriously undertaken, confirmed, and prayed about can never fail. Irrespective of the fact that this is a problematic way to handle Scripture, this kind of denominational victory narrative creates a positively toxic environment for pioneer church plants. It needs to be restated that the goal of pioneer church planting isn't simply to form a church; it is to also to explore new ways of being the church. This requires that the church plant balance both the task of creating something new with the task of becoming a church. If failure isn't an option then pioneer church planting isn't for your tribe. Again I would urge you, for the sake of your denomination's planting department, and for the sake of the ministry of pioneer planters, it would be better to refer pioneer planters to another group.

Denominations should make a considered and thoughtful examination of their culture before deciding to engage with pioneer church planters. A mismatch in culture can cause unnecessary tension, conflict, and even closures in pioneer church plants. A mismatch negatively impacts the life of the church plant, and in the worst cases can rob the Canadian context of future church plants by permanently sidelining a pioneer planter. This is a price the church in Canada cannot afford to continue paying.

Please ensure before you engage with pioneer church plants that your denominational culture can handle the pressure. Here are a couple of questions to help get started in some denominational self-examination:

- Does our denomination include a significant diversity of church forms already?
- Does our diversity include communities from distinctive Canadian subcultures (bikers, hipsters, urban, suburban, rural, Star Trek fans, etc.) and people from other ethnicities?

Evidence of already-existing diversity suggests that your denomination has done the hard work of adjusting itself in order to unify, support, and nurture people who are "different." The fact that your group contains *both* Canadian subcultural groups and immigrant churches means that your denomination sees Canada clearly. All too often the term "different" is reserved solely for people groups born elsewhere. This kind of cultural blindness creates a double standard. Immigrant churches under these conditions are free to be different. They are free to adjust how they do things in order to meet the needs of their people. Conversely, churches serving the needs of people born in Canada are often not as free. In denominations like these, there is often an unstated expectation that all churches that serve the needs of people born in Canada should essentially look and operate in the same way. If your denomination hasn't done the hard work of adjusting to difference in all its Canadian forms, there is a good chance your group won't be ready to support pioneer church planting. Heed the words of this planter:

"I would not say that my denomination supports new and evolving forms of church. They support immigrant churches and the classic, white, come-to-our-soft-launch, evangelical, seeker-sensitive, wear-jeans-look-cool churches."

The new Canadian reality is that culture matters. The future of our country means more diversity, not less. The work of adjusting to our surroundings, and adjusting how we do things in order to meet the needs of the people around us is real work. This is pathfinder work. If your denomination does not already contain this diversity you may find pioneer church plants to be more than you can handle.

Here are some other questions to help you with denominational self-awareness:

- Has our denomination ever changed its mode of operating, by-laws and policies, or other denominational systems to better accommodate new forms of church?
- Does our denomination often express a need and a desire for new ways of being the church?
- Do we invite pioneer planters to help us shape our current church planting processes around assessment, training, coaching, networking, and funding?
- How much "down field blocking" do we need to do to protect pioneer church plants?
- How would we rate our denomination's overall need to "get" what is going on in every church plant?
- Does not understanding what a church plant is bother us?
- Has our denomination ever sat down in a formal way to ask "what is our ecclesiology now"?

Invest Where It Counts

Another suggestion from our planters was for denominations to take a closer look at the investing of their financial resources. Surprisingly, the planters weren't asking for larger salaries. In fact, it seemed that most were resigned, from the get-go, to the fact that their planting work would not be their sole source of income. Bi-vocational ministry appears to be the norm for pioneers, but more research needs to be done to determine if this represents a good thing, a bad thing, or both for pioneer planting. At this point we can only observe that it is the experience of the majority. Interestingly, the planters in this study suggested that denominations focus their finances on resourcing over paying salaries. Here's how one participant put it:

"Stop paying [church planters'] salaries. Don't insist that they go to assessment to figure out whether or not they can plant. Send them to things that can hone their skills and craft. Put your money into preparing them the best you can. Give them everything you can to resource and help them."

I don't think this participant is suggesting that nothing should go toward church planter salaries or that assessments are completely unhelpful. Instead, I interpret this to mean that skill development should be a significant area of focus for denominational resources. The suggestion here seems two-fold. First, pioneer planters need training and resourcing. This could include things like training events, conferences, and other professional development opportunities. Another suggestion would be to invest in opportunities for planters to develop job skills that make the bi-vocational life a little less onerous. It could mean investing in things like book and software allowances. Most cash-strapped church plants consider these sorts of expenses as "someday items," especially when these items are placed against budgets lines like paying rent. Second, pioneer plants would benefit if denominations invest in cultivating and supporting church planting networks. One participant said, *"Having the right network around you is as important as getting your finances in place. You need people who will applaud and support and also push back."* The power of peer networks is instrumental in developing sustainable planting in the Canadian context. There is real loneliness when it comes to planting, and the value of having others around you is high. One participant put it this way:

> *"Plant a church. Don't worry about cash. Pay more attention to surrounding yourself with friends and mentors who have been there before you."*

These are some pretty stark comments about the need to be surrounded and supported. Planters often express a sense of loneliness, and it could very well be that networks are a part of the cure. Denominations should take all of this into account in their church planting budgets.

The planter's comment about assessment above is another area which denominations should carefully consider. I want to point out that many of the planters in this study went through a planter's assessment of one kind or another. For many it was a poor experience. Even planters that passed their assessments had negative things to say about the process. I think this merits a second look.

One thing to consider is how your denomination approaches assessment. Here's a set of key questions: who is assessment primarily for? Is it there to protect your denomination? Or, is it there to ensure that planters enter into this work deeply confident that they have heard from God and are ready to respond? The needs of your denomination and the needs of your planters don't have to be mutually exclusive. That being said, denominations that prioritize their own protection over the needs of their planters shouldn't be surprised if planters aren't feeling empowered by the process. In the long run, denominations may find that making planter confidence and preparation primary is a better way forward. By prioritizing the needs of planters they may find this approach has many of the same outcomes as the defensive approach but with the added benefit of empowered planters.

A second thing to consider is the reason that church plants come into being. Is a church plant born because of a set of skills and behaviours? Or does it come about because the planter feels caught up in a certain story? In typical pastoral ministry the former option is more often assumed. Generally, a person who feels called by God to be a pastor enters pastoral ministry with a unique set of strengths, abilities, and weaknesses. The church in which they are candidating will come to the table with a sense of what strengths and skills they are looking for in a leader. The potential pastor and congregation will prayerfully and carefully consider their respective lists and look for a good match. The same doesn't seem to hold true for planting. I have yet to encounter planters who use a gifts-based approach to determining the neighbourhood they will plant in or the people group they work among. Rather, a planter's choices and motivations seem to come less from their skills and abilities and more from a story they feel is unfolding in their lives. If, as a denomination, your chosen assessment method is more gifts- and abilities-oriented than it is story-oriented, you may want to consider a new method.

Third, ask some specific questions of the assumptions underlying your chosen assessment methodology as a denomination. Does it assume either of the following statements? 1) We know what kind of church planting needs to take place in all the subcultures in Canada, or 2) we can describe and identify the kind of leader needed to plant these various kinds of churches. These are some pretty big assumptions given the challenges the church faces in the current Canadian context. Some of the negativity the planters in the study expressed about assessment seemed to arise from a rejection of these assumptions. They often felt like they were being squeezed into a mold. You should listen to them. If your assessment method buys into these assumptions your denomination's church planting system will be limited. Your future will be confined to the kinds of church plants and planters your assessment method allows you to "see." You are, in effect, reducing the possible directions and areas of Canadian culture that your denomination can move into. Based on the statements of planters in this study I think we owe it to them to have a serious and sober second look at the way our denominations do planter assessment.

Create an Authentic Partnership

It may also surprise you, given the non-joiner reputation of church planters, that most of the planters in this study expressed a genuine desire for partnership with their denomination. These planters saw belonging to a denomination as foundational to what they were trying to accomplish. One participant's word to other planters was, *"One of the things you can't do anymore is go it alone."* Others expressed a high level of satisfaction with their experience in their denomination thus far, saying things like:

> *"Our denomination believes in us. I think that goes a long way. I don't believe we work at crossed purposes with the denomination that we are loved in. We may go at things in a different manner, but the main things are the main things. And we don't have any sense that we are left adrift."*

All of this points to the possibility for meaningful partnership between pioneer planters and denominations. That's good news for the future of both!

When it comes to partnerships between denominations and planters the best way forward is to seek out an authentic partnership. Authentic partnerships have several markers, the first being harmony in vision. While you may not share all things in common, one thing you do share is a common vision for the future. Denominations that seek genuine partnerships with the plants in their care should be clear about their vision and ask specific questions about the vision of the church plant they want to partner with. Second, authentic partnerships require mutuality—there must be mutual benefit in the partnership. This means that each partner brings something important to the table. There must also be acknowledged mutuality of need, meaning that some key thing is missing in both parties that the other party can fill. Anything less than this and the relationship devolves to ownership. For instance, the party with money tends to own the party that needs money. Needless to say, this kind of arrangement doesn't easily lead to authentic partnership.

Unfortunately, ownership is a common way that denominations and church plants relate to each other. The planters in this study desired something more. Speaking myself as a denominational leader, we want something more as well. It is important that both groups take these desires seriously and invest energy in creating something more.

Navigate the Unexplored World of Aftercare

If you accept the premise of this study that pioneer church plants experience additional risk, then it follows that failure will be common. If denominations want to responsibly engage with pioneer church plants, they will need a concrete plan for aftercare if a plant does not continue. This would be advisable for any denomination involved in any kind of church planting but it is especially important for those engage with pioneer church plants. I will be delving more deeply into this matter in the next chapter, but for now I want to highlight a couple of helpful ideas in developing an aftercare plan.

One essential ingredient in developing an aftercare plan is simply to do it. Planters reported to me that my interview request, which in many cases happened several years after their project had finished, was the first time they had ever had an official conversation about what happened. I think this is tragic to say the least. Church plants will close—that is a fact. It is important for us to think about what our response as denominations will be when, not if this does occur. So what does responding well look like?

The primary response should be one of recognition. It is important to recognize several things. The first is that the planter engaged in the project with genuine and honest effort. Secondly, the failure was likely unexpected and so the planter may be asking some foundational questions about their worth, skill, and calling as leaders. Thirdly, the planter is likely facing disappointment in themselves and perhaps even in God. Acknowledging these things may not be comfortable but it is important nonetheless. Your goal in your response as a denomination should be to recognize the effort, the risk, the faith, and the courage that it takes just to try something new. Planters are gutsy people. You can recognize that the depth of the planter's disappointment demonstrates the "all in" attitude they brought to the project. Finally, you can recognize the simple truth that God isn't done with them yet. It may be unclear, and even too early to talk about what the future holds, but it is important that they know that there is one.

Another essential ingredient in developing an aftercare plan is to create space for learning. Have the planter tell you their story in depth. Treat them not as a failure but as an expert. After all, a pioneer has been to places your denomination hasn't been before. Ask them what they learned from their experience. Ask them what advice they might have for other planters that were thinking some of the same things. Ask them if they have any advice for you as a leader or as a denomination. All of this is important because if denominations cannot learn from previous attempts, they will never progress in their capacity to find new ways of being the church.

Yet another essential ingredient in developing an aftercare plan is to pay attention to time. It is important to realize that some planters won't be able to talk about their experience right away. They might be embarrassed, hurt, angry, or feeling any number of other emotions. Initial contact should be around appreciation and recognition of what they attempted. Keep it simple. For the planter, fully understanding and processing what happened will take some time—in some cases, years. If you seek to be a learning community as a denomination, you will need to revisit their story when they are ready.

Finally, be open to the planter trying again. Quite honestly this will be the single greatest test of your denomination's willingness to support pioneer church plants. If you are unwilling to do this, you should refer all future pioneer planters to a denomination that will. Planters that have tried and failed—and if they recover, choose to learn from what happened, and want to do it again—are invaluable to your denomination. In fact, they may even have more to offer you than a planter that has only ever succeeded. Why? Because failure, unlike success, naturally leads to re-evaluate our unexamined assumptions. When things go according to plan we seldom ask "Why?" Instead, we are prone to jump straight to "How can we do that again?" A denomination that does not reflect on why things do or don't work is missing vital information. Failures can force us to ask hard questions about our assumptions in ways that successes never will. What denominations learn from this process makes for solid material in building a learning community.

Denominations have an important role to play in the ongoing health of pioneer church plants in Canada. The good news is that the experience of many pioneer church planters has been positive. Generally speaking, denominations in Canada are providing an adequate level of support or at least getting out of the way. However, planters did make some important suggestions concerning how to increase the level of support from their denominations. Their first suggestion was that denominations evaluate their capacity to support pioneer planting in the first place. Denominations with a strong need for control have less capacity than those that are more open and flexible. Their second suggestion was that denominations invest more financially in the area of resourcing. Their third suggestion was that denominations pursue authentic partnerships with their planters, ensuring that both parties have harmony of vision and mutuality in terms of benefit and need. Finally, the stories of our planters suggested that denominations have a long way to go in the area of providing aftercare. In order to do this well, denominations need to recognize the effort and faith of planters. They need to learn from their experiences. They need to take their time. And finally they need to be open to planters trying again. Increasing denominational capacity for supporting and nurturing pioneer church plants in Canada means that we can leave the door open for something new to emerge in our Canadian context. The pathfinder's road isn't an easy one and there is much that denominations can do to support them along the way.

14

God Ain't Done With You Yet

Planters can and do recover from when a church plant doesn't continue.

> *"Would I do it all over again, knowing how it ended?*
> *I would do it all over again, including if the hurt and*
> *pain had to be a part of doing it all over again."*

U p until this point, we have been talking about what steps church planters can take to ensure their plants continue for years to come. We've looked at all kinds of factors and lifesaving information that plays into the development of a healthy church plant. In one sense this book is about helping you to avoid needing to read this chapter. All the same, this book wouldn't be complete without it. The fact remains that you could follow all of the hard-won advice in these pages and still wind up leading a church that doesn't survive. Church planting doesn't have any guarantees—that's the sad reality of it. And yet, sadder still is the thought that things not working out means the end of the road for many church planters. This is downright tragic. It's a tragedy because church planters are a rare breed—and pioneer church planters even more so. The fact is that the Canadian church simply cannot afford to have any more church planters permanently sidelined. Failure will happen, we don't have a choice in the matter, but that doesn't mean a planter should never plant again. That's an area where we do have a choice.

This was one of the most difficult chapters to write in this book. The feelings here are raw. One participant described going through a church plant closure like this: *"I felt hurt, desperate, broken and beat up and that I had been wasting my life for years."* The emotional stakes are high because planters pray their guts out, place their faith in the idea that God is asking them to do something crazy, step out to do something about it, and invite others along for the ride. Planting only works if you go all in, and planting failure hurts precisely because you went all in. Listen to this planter's experience:

"When the doors shut, and you go home and you've got nothing to do on a Sunday, that is really hard to deal with on an emotional, spiritual, and psychological level."

Failure can be devastating, confusing, and faith-shaking. In another planter's words:

"The thing with this kind of work is that a piece of your heart is in there. And it never goes away. Never."

The wounds can go deep. Closure can burn you right down to the foundations of who you think you are, what you believe, and what you value. But, hear me out, I am trying to walk a fine line here. On one hand, I want to represent reality in as unvarnished a way as possible because the truth is instructive. On the other hand, I don't want to discourage any future planter from stepping out in faith and being obedient to God. I also don't want you to believe that you only get one shot at this as a planter.

Many of the participants in this study insisted that I tell planters who have experienced church closure loud and clear, "God ain't done with you yet." They want you to know that the recovery process, while often hard and often taking longer than you want it to, *can* lead to new ministry. They wanted me to tell you that recovery is not only possible but, if you take their advice, even likely!

Let's explore the steps that some of the planters in this study took to recover when their plants didn't continue.

Processing Your Emotions

Okay, let's start here: this is going to hurt. There's no getting around it, and no use in pretending. I repeat: this is going to hurt. It will hurt because you cared. It will hurt because you tried. It will hurt because you'll have given it all you had. Don't be in a big hurry to move past the pain part. The pain is real and it's to be expected. The first step in the recovery process is to live out the emotions that arise from the closure of your plant. Processing emotions follows a few basic steps: the first is to notice your emotions, next to identify them, next to make sense of them, and then finally to decide how you will cope with what you feel. Let's trace these steps through one of the stories from the study to see this process in action.

Remember when I said expect the unexpected? Changes in your life circumstances may be the reason for the closure of your church plant. In one of the cases in the study it was the unexpected arrival of a child that meant that the planter family was no longer able to live and minister in the neighbourhood in which they planted. They couldn't afford a bigger place to live, and the plant depended on their remaining in the neighbourhood, so they couldn't stay onboard as leaders. They wrestled for months over their decision to pull the plug on their involvement. Eventually they were offered a church position in a neighbouring city where they could afford to live as a family. Listen to the planter's words:

"I felt like a sell-out. Here I was, believing so passionately in church planting and living the urban life in a city and I was about to move out to the suburbs, buy a house, and work at an established church full-time. And yet at the same time I didn't feel like I could put my family through another year."

The decision to go never comes easily. It can be agonizing, especially when you start throwing around phrases like "sell-out." There's a smoke-laced thought. It comes from the pit. That isn't the voice of your Father talking—it's accusatory. It's black-and-white thinking. It's dealing in absolutes. So how do you recover from secretly worrying you are sell-out?

The first step is to notice what you're feeling. Stare at it. Ask your feelings to make their case. Many dark thoughts do not enjoy being directly in the light; they prefer remaining as unthought thoughts, unexamined and unarticulated ideas hovering just outside your consciousness. The work of examining what you're feeling is what Paul refers to when he encourages Christians to "take captive every thought to make it obedient to Christ" (2 Corinthians 10:5). The first step in recovery for a discouraged planter is learning how to arrest your thoughts and bring them in for questioning. Once you have them in the interrogation room, see how you might make them obedient to Christ. In the case of the participant above, the struggle took time. There were long-suffering, self-sacrificial attempts to stay. However, staying, after a while, was motivated more by the fear of being a sell-out than a clear directive from God. That thought needed an arrest—it had to be brought in for questioning, and it had to face facts. If staying was not an option, then what was? This is the beautiful thing about bringing our thoughts under God's authority: it can eventually open up options for us. Sell-outs are motivated by fear; they always take the path of least resistance. People who face facts, prayerfully consider what God might be saying to them, and then act according to what they hear have options. They are free to imagine what is possible now.

Here is how this particular story ended: with a well-adjusted pastor. The world he lived in while he was planting was neatly divided into sell-outs and heroes. Now the lines are less sharp and he has found himself more patient with others, more humble in his estimation of himself, and more capable of leading real people in a real direction. In his care is an established congregation that is sympathetic and supportive of pioneer church planting efforts. This congregation now engages with its neighbourhood in a way it wouldn't have if it were it not for the planting experience of its leader. Many of the folks from the initial church plant have moved on to other faith communities, and their planting experience is informing and shaping their new communities as well. Not bad! It's hard to really call this whole experience a failure.

Without a community with whom to process emotions, planters are on their own. Under these circumstance it can be easy for planters to get stuck. They can spend years in a loop of self-loathing, bitterness, anger, resentment or worse. For some, being a church planter is tied to a sense of self-worth. When they are no longer planting, they feel empty. One participant, years after their plant closed, still wondered:

"I often think I've taken my best shot and I'll never be anything significant again. Are my best years behind me?"

Leave such thoughts and feelings long enough and these wounds can lead to outright hatred for other Christians or develop into an unresolved suspicion of God. Properly processing emotions is vital to the ongoing spiritual and mental health of planters.

Processing the Spiritual Fallout

The failure of a church plant is not only an emotional journey but a spiritual one as well. After all, planters begin the process with a sense that God is behind it all. They see confirmation after confirmation as the plant begins to take shape. As others join, faith and confidence grows in the fact that God is behind all of this. When a church plant fails, everything can be called into question. Did God really speak? Did I hear correctly? Were we all deceived? Was failure God's plan? How can I trust Him again? Does He even exist? If questions like these remain unattended, the effects on faith can be permanent. However, the good news from the study is that permanent damage isn't inevitable. Many planters in this study demonstrated the ability to get their faith back on track. They talked about redemptive moments and God's grace. In some cases they even reported stronger faith and character than they'd had before they planted. As with processing our emotions there are stages and steps to processing things on a spiritual level. This work requires honesty, and inviting God and others in. In time, it will mean rehabilitating your faith muscles and moving into what God has for you next.

So let's start at the beginning. How can planters be honest about what has happened from a spiritual point of view? Here is how one planter described this first phase:

> *"I was lost. I didn't have a job. I didn't have a church. I had a relationship with God but I felt like I had failed Him and myself and my family. I had debt. I was alone. It was really a dark time."*

This was a common starting point for many planters: feeling as though they'd let God down. What's worse is that this kind of thinking can lead you to believe that God doesn't want anything to do with you or that He has abandoned you. While we clearly know that this doesn't line up with the character of God, it can become an irresistible idea to a discouraged planter. So this is where the work needs to start for planters: noticing where you are at and having the courage to name what you are tempted to believe about God. Faking it or pretending doesn't help. Once you can own what you believe, the next challenge is to actually allow God and others into that reality. Some participants found it helpful at this point to form questions they wanted to ask God. One planter put it like this:

> *"In my journey with God I needed to find out if I was done or not—to find out whether or not I was a church planter. And that journey continues to this day."*

The questions planters ask under these circumstances seem to come in two basic forms. The first concerns a planter's own worth. Questions in this stage can be: God, am I still good? Do I still have worth? Do you still love me? The second concerns God's worth. Questions in this stage can be: God, are You still good? Were You ever? Do You even exist or am I just talking to myself? What we know from God's character is that the safest place for our doubts is in His hands. He knows His way around the human heart and He isn't afraid. Planters who are able to be honest about their spiritual condition do better than those who avoid dealing with it.

I don't want to leave the impression that processing the spiritual fallout resulting from a non-continuing church plant is all doom and gloom; there are plenty of redemption stories out there. God can and does meet planters in their need, and their lives and character are transformed as a result. Here's how one planter described their experience:

> *"It has caused me to have a little less confidence. I was one of those church planters who said church planting was easy. How hard could it be? You go over there, you do a bunch of stuff, and people come. My experience has shown me that if God's not in it, or if I'm not up to the task, I really can fail. So it's been a really good experience that way. It's been a humbling experience."*

Although it may not feel like it, sometimes a little less confidence can be a good thing. This is especially true if your personality often veers dangerously into arrogance. Facing your deepest spiritual fears is not a gift or situation any of us would voluntarily walk through. That being said, many participants reported transformation and redemption at the end. Spiritual wounds may be hard to deal with – but they don't need to be fatal.

Remember That You Are Not Alone

This study revealed a giant hole in the Canadian church's collective ability to cope with church plant closures: namely, the fact that the suffering of church planter spouses often goes unnoticed. Church planter spouses suffer the emotional and spiritual grief of a church plant closure alongside their spouse.

However, while they share the experience, they often cope much differently. I regret deeply that I was not able to delve more into this important story—this might be my next research project. While I am not fully satisfied with my understanding of these realities, I thought I would share what I did gather from the interviews.

For one, it is important that planters recognize that their spouses and children will need time to process their emotional and spiritual wounds too. Depending on the emotional and spiritual makeup of a planter's spouse and children, this will look different from person to person. What was said in the last two sections on emotional and spiritual health processing may apply to them as well. Openness and honesty are important starting points, and so is inviting God and others into the story to help.

One kind of grief that a planter's spouse and children may not be prepared to process is the social loss that a church plant closure represents. Here is how one spouse described it to me:

"When it was over, it was extremely painful. It was the loss of something we had birthed and all of the wonderful friends we'd had."

The loss of community can be profound for your family—pay attention.

A planter must exercise care and sensitivity around the thoughts and feelings of their family after a plant closure. There were several cases in this study in which the planter had recovered to the point of being willing to try again but the family hadn't. Planters in this situation must be patient. It will do no one any good to force this issue, and you can't rush healing. One spouse described their feelings like this:

"It has torn my heart to feel as though I failed these people and to watch what happened to the community and my

children subsequently. I would never put myself in that situation again. Never."

Feelings like these should never be dismissed, treated lightly, or stepped over in an effort to get on to the next project. As a planter, remember that you planted together with your spouse. You'll need to recover together. Don't ignore your family, and don't let them walk alone in silence with their wounds untreated. Pay attention and be patient. Invite God and others into your situation to help.

Remember That There is Future

If you are right in the middle of processing the loss of your church plant it can be hard to imagine that anything good could ever come from something so painful. While this is an understandable thought, the good news is that this isn't the whole story. Understandably, all of the participants with non-continuing churches found the whole process incredibly difficult. But what I found surprising was the number of planters who, despite the pain, discovered benefits in the process.

Some found that their church planting experience played a huge role in their future ministry. One participant noted, *"what happened in our city will travel with us forever. It was very formative."* Even though this particular planter's involvement ended years ago, and they now work far from the city where they planted, their church planting experience has impacted them deeply. There are possibilities that church planting can open up for planters that other kinds of ministry cannot deliver. If you are able to process your feelings and the spiritual dimensions of your experience as a planter, there is potential for God to use your experience in amazing ways. Maybe it will even be in your next church plant?!

Another benefit planters described from walking through this process is that it provided an opportunity for personal growth. That is quite a statement, given that this process is often one of the most difficult moments in their ministry life!

To this day, a number of planters remain committed to church planting. They are an active support to others who are exploring planting, they are a coach, and they are active in marshalling any resources they have to see church planting move forward in their city. Others saw how the church planting experience has confirmed this person's gifting and deepened their understanding of their calling. *"I wouldn't do anything differently because this is who I am,"* said this planter.

Church planters, especially pioneer church planters, are far too valuable to be permanently benched just because a project doesn't turn out. It is vitally important that the Canadian church find ways of helping planters process their grief, sense of loss, and embarrassment when things don't work out. The help we offer will need to take into consideration the emotional and spiritual toll of the experience of a church closure. We'll need to think, not just in terms of planters, but in terms of their families as well. Finally, it is important to have networks in which these kinds of stories are shared and celebrated. Perhaps if we take the possibility of failure seriously, and if we refrain from shaming those who experience it, we could do more to soften the sting and stigma. Perhaps if we work in this way, we'll have more veteran church planters around to help us move into the future.

15

A One-Shot Deal?

The future of pioneer church planting in Canada depends on planters who can overcome their reluctance to plant more than once.

"The challenge [of sustaining a church planting movement] is the people who have already planted or are planting. How do you convince them not to just settle? Because it is a lot of work to plant. Three years ago I was physically just done in. So the challenge is, how do you get people past that?"

Wouldn't it make sense that the best candidates for the future of pioneer church planting in Canada would be people who have attempted it at least once before? Wouldn't the future be safer in the hands of people who have a realistic vision of what pioneer church planting involves? Wouldn't we all benefit if we had veteran planters piloting our future plants because they knew where some of the rocky shoals were? I believe we would.

The challenge for our collective future is that this doesn't seem to be happening. Our veterans are, by and large, sitting this next round out. Here is how the numbers broke down in this study. Of the 19 planters interviewed only 11 said *yes, they would plant again*. Of those 11, only 5 had any concrete plans to do so. The remaining 6 of the 11 said yes but in a more or less foggy, "someday" kind of way. Of the 8 that didn't say yes, 4 said *maybe they would plant again.* The remaining 4 said that *they would not consider planting again.* The following response was typical for most:

> *"I can't see myself ever planting again, but I would support someone else. I would get involved but I wouldn't plant a new church myself."*

So, at least up until now, pioneer church planting seems to be a one-shot deal. This is a giant loss for the church in Canada. So what gives? How do improve our chances that veterans will plant more than once? Here are a few suggestions.

The first step to improving our chances is understanding why pioneer church planters are reluctant to plant again. The answers here are as varied as the individual but that doesn't mean that there aren't themes. I noted at least three.

The first theme is the high cost of planting to a planter's family. Quite simply, the planter doesn't want to put their family through the experience again. This response wasn't limited to participants who had experienced family breakdowns or had their church plants close. One participant, whose plant is still continuing, put it like this: *"... at this stage in my kids' lives, we've already brought them through a lot..."* The barriers to re-entry are obviously even higher for those who don't fare as well as he did. Part of making church planting a repeatable thing lies with the planter and their family and their ability to process the challenges and costs of planting again. The other half of the equation lies with those who are responsible for planter systems and networks. We need to sit up here and pay attention to this phenomenon. More focused research and thought on the strain of planting on the planter's family is needed. Planting systems and networks also need to commit to acting on those findings. One participant suggested that the future of pioneer planting depends on denominations making sure that families are *"provided for so that stressors can be handled with wisdom."* If we choose to ignore these realities, pioneer church planting in this country will only ever be a one-shot deal, at best. At worst, our ignorance of what they are going through will play a role in the destruction of marriages and families.

The second theme of a reluctance to plant again concerned incomplete processing of the emotional and spiritual costs of pioneer church planting. You'll notice I didn't say "the emotional and spiritual costs of a church plant closing." The costs are not limited to planters of non-continuing churches—everyone who engages in pioneer church planting pays an emotional and spiritual toll. Succeed or fail, pioneer church planting leaves planters exhausted and depleted. In many cases, including ones where things turned out all right, recovery can take years. Once again, I want to suggest that we all need to enter into church planting, as planters, denominations, and networks, with our eyes wide open. Even under ideal conditions, church planting is hard. Let's be ready for this and take all the steps we can to help our planters manage the costs.

A third theme I found concerning the reluctance of pioneer planters to plant again is that a handful of these planters did not, in the end, think that they were church planters. You read that right. Some of the participants in this study, who planted churches, did not see themselves as church planters. How could this be? There are several possible explanations. The first may be that they meant to convey that they see themselves as church founders and not lifelong planters. A lifelong planter is someone who moves from planting project to planting project as their life vocation. A founder is someone who feels uniquely called to a neighbourhood for life. So the thought of moving into a different neighbourhood was not part of their imagined future. A second possible explanation may be that our current definition of a planter may need an update. The current fantasy image of planters as rootless alpha males moving from place to place, drawing people around them with raw charismatic power and single-handedly carrying the church on their backs is problematic to say the least. It is possible that some of the participants might have defined a true church planter in this way and therefore discounted themselves from future attempts. They just didn't fit the type. I want to suggest that if this is our definition of a planter then we have a serious problem. As a result of this study I am less and less convinced that planting should be seen as the work of an individual rootless alpha male. There are several things wrong with this picture. First, we need both men and women to step up and become pioneer planters. Some of the maladies of the churches in this study may have been due to the fact that this was almost an exclusively male enterprise. We need more research to dig into this further. Second, limiting pioneer church planting to a single personality type is a problematic construct. The participants in this study proved that pioneer church planting can be done by all kinds of people. Thirdly, church planting leadership shouldn't be limited to one person. There is far too much at stake and the work is far too heavy to leave in the hands of an individual. Foruthly, we need better models. We need better ways of working, a better understanding of what a church is, and how church plants should be led. We need this for no other reason than to make it possible for normal people to plant more than once.

Now, I want to be careful here. I want to keep my work rooted in what I observed. The theories in this book are meant to be grounded ones, rising out the soil of what is, not what could be. The plants I interviewed for this project were almost exclusively lead by solo planters. Yes, some had strong teams. Yes, some were very collaborative in how they operated. Yes, some went to incredible lengths to share power and leadership. And yet, with few exceptions, the dominant leadership model and survival spark for these church plants was very much rooted in the gifted individual. Where we go from here will need to be left up to future pioneers who can point the way. Once we have more examples to learn from we can begin learning and shaping new definitions—hopefully ones that bear repeating.

So what can planters, denominational leaders, and networks do about the reluctance we currently see among planters to plant again? I think we have at least two ways to move forward.

The first step, which probably won't feel like a step at all, will be to wait. We need to have patience as planters recover from the first their attempt. Whether the church plant continued or not, recovery will take time, and their story is still developing. Some planters who currently don't see themselves planting again may change their minds—only time will tell. Returning to action before they are ready does not seem like a winning strategy, so we must wait and see what happens.

The second step we need to take is to pray. I know that this can sound trite, but the truth is that we need a breakthrough in Canada. There are limits to what our current systems can do, and limits to the kind of supports we can offer. There are also limits to what a planter can do, manage, and control. Almost all of the participants in the study said that they would re-enter the church planting world if they felt God calling them to it. So I think this is a good place to start. If some of the participants are waiting for a call from God, then let's pray that He will call them back into the fray. Obviously, God is in charge of who He calls and what He calls them to. We don't have enough information to be doing this ourselves. Some participants said that they now feel called to the neighbourhood they are currently serving. It will need to be up to God if He wants to call them somewhere else. Some feel called to their current work of coaching and supporting church planters directly. They may not be on the frontlines at the moment, but their work is still important. We need to leave it up to God as to how and where He deploys His people. However nothing should prevent us from fasting and praying that God would send more workers into His harvest fields. Nothing should prevent us from praying that God would finish His healing work in the lives of these veterans and call and release them into future ministry. Nothing should prevent us from praying that God would break through and burn away the sense of failure, the sense of shame, the sense of inadequacy, the fears, and the exhaustion that some of these pioneer planters are experiencing. Nothing should prevent us from asking God for what we need to see the influence of Jesus and His kingdom spread in Canada. The apostle James, when he reflected on life with God warned us, "You do not have because you do not ask God" (James 4:2). Could it be that one of the reasons we don't see more veteran church planters back in the game is because we have not asked God for that?

In the end we need to understand that the full story of the churches in the *One Size Fits All?* documentary hasn't been written yet. We need to do more to understand why pioneer planters seem reluctant to do this kind of work more than once. We need to sit up and take notice. We need to do a better job of understanding what happens in the family systems of pioneer planters as they do this kind of work. We need to take seriously and act upon what we might learn. We need to understand more about the emotional and spiritual costs associated with pioneer church planting. We need to further explore what we mean when we imagine and define what a church planter is and does. A feeling that they don't measure up may be partially responsible for the hesitation of experienced planters who are waiting this next round out. This research project is a good start as an exploration of some of these questions, but we need to go deeper. We need to create better support systems and networks that do a better job of nurturing and supporting planters and their families. We need to have patience as the real work of recovery takes time. Finally, we need to pray to the Lord of the harvest that He will send the workers needed to bring in the Canadian harvest. We have a God-sized challenge ahead of us and we'll need a God-sized answer. It's time to start asking.

16

Conclusion

Where it all might go...

"I think that this project is more important than we realize. We need Canadian stories. Our identity has to arise from something other than not being American. There are great things happening in towns and cities in this country and we don't seem to be good at celebrating that."

Over the last number of years, there has been a lot of pioneer church planting going on in Canada. I hope that these pages have done something to ensure that these stories don't disappear. The good news is that I currently think that forgetting these stories isn't likely to happen! God is up to something new and there seems to be fresh appetite for planting new kinds of churches.

I'm not the only one who has noticed that something new is blossoming in our country. The Spirit seems to be seeding Canadian cities and towns with a new kind of people who are wanting to form a new way of life together—a new way of being the church. What's so mind-blowing is that these new kinds of people belong to all kinds of different denominations, align with different theologies and doctrines, and are being shaped by distinct histories and traditions. Differences are nothing new, but what is new is that there is a growing kinship, a connection, and a "getting it" among this diverse group of people. All this despite the fact that they don't all live in the same area, read the same books, belong to the same denomination, or necessarily even hold all the same ideas about God. Yet there is something they hold in common that just can't be denied. When this kinship first emerged, it inspired the *One Size Fits All?* documentary. Now in its second bloom, it's what is inspiring the writing of this book. I didn't write this book to commemorate the past; I wanted to support the future. This second bloom of something new is also catalyzing the formation of a new conversation in Canada called the "New Leaf Network."

Imagine this:

What if pioneer planters, as a kinship community, when we first blossomed, had organized ourselves so that we connected with and invested in each other more? For starters, books like this would not have been necessary. Why? Because we would already have known these stories. We would have easily absorbed the emerging principles and themes and would have put them to good use. These days I actively wonder if more of our early pioneers would still be with us today if we had organized—not because their pioneering work would have continued but because they wouldn't have had to walk through their disappointment alone. How would their journey have been different if they'd had a network that was proud of them simply for trying something new? How would their journey have been different if they'd had a community who understood firsthand the kind of risk and faith it takes to step out and follow Jesus into pioneer planting? How would their journey have been different if they'd had a network that helped them make sense of what happened, helped them pick up the pieces, and insisted that they carry on? If we'd had a network, perhaps, for a few at least, it wouldn't have been the first and last time they attempted to plant.

As for myself and small group of stout-hearted folks, we are starting to do more than just wonder. We are actively banding together to see what a network might be capable of. The New Leaf Network is the result of our work.

The goal of the New Leaf Network is to nurture and support pioneer planters as they live out their calling in the Canadian context. We want to see an environment where pioneer planters have personal, theological, and practical support through relationships both locally and across Canada. We are a group of denominations, networks, and churches that believe we are better together. We believe first and foremost that pioneer work needs to be attempted across Canada—our collective futures depend on it. We also know that pioneer planting won't be easy. In light of this, we are investing in gathering together to ensure that pioneer planting continues in our country. We want to become a learning community. We want to learn to ask better questions about the Canadian context and what it will take to put the gospel within reach of all the people who live here. We want to develop underlying principles and practices that make pioneer work as simple, safe, successful, and repeatable as possible. We want to make it more attractive for ourselves and others to try something new in Canada.

To build this network is going to take time, energy, and focus. Being together isn't easy—it takes work. For pioneer planters, it will be especially difficult. Many planters are deeply in love with and entrenched in their neighbourhoods; lifting their heads up to see a regional—let alone a national—horizon is hard. It will at times even seem counter-intuitive, but it will still be important. Our collective future in Canada depends on it. I hope the stories in this book do something to develop our collective sense of urgency around this. Canada may be geographically large but it is still a small place. There isn't a very large group of people attempting pioneer church planting here. Distance from each other and developing critical mass makes developing a national conversation really tough. It will cost us something to be together.

So that's where you come in, dear reader. There must have been a reason you picked this book up in the first place. Perhaps it's because you have a growing sense that God is asking you to start a new kind of church. Perhaps you're a denominational leader and you know and support pioneer planters. Perhaps you're just an interested listener and you wanted to know more. Whatever the reason, I ask that you would consider a few things as a response to having read this book.

The first would be to pray for us. The work of this network and the people that we support are engaged in an inherently aggressive act. We are pushing against the kingdom of this world and attempting to establish outposts deep behind enemy lines. We not only appreciate your prayers but desperately need them. The second would be to join the conversation. If you are considering doing something new in Canada, if you are feeling called not only to establish a new church, but a new kind of church, then please don't do it alone—join us. If we are hosting an event in your area, I'd like to invite you to pull up a chair and join us. If you see us post something on Facebook, interact with us. Share the conversation we're having with others. If you run across our podcast "The New Leaf Project" give us a listen and interact with us. Send us ideas for stories that we should be telling. If you run across our blog, consider commenting or maybe even contributing an article yourself. We have a lot of dialogue ahead of us as we get our bearings and your participation will mean a lot to us. If your denominational leaders have never heard of us, please let them know that we exist. Ask them to support your participation in the network and to consider becoming an active partner with us as we grow. The third would be to consider actively supporting us with either your time, your talent, or your finances. We will need all kinds of help in getting ourselves established. We'll need help from coast to coast. Get in touch with us through our website or through Facebook, Twitter or other social media outlets and let us know you are interested.

Friends, neither the New Leaf Network nor this book existed when myself or my friends were getting started. I hope that you find in these pages some encouragement, some inspiration, some ideas, and some warnings. This kind of work is life-changing. This kind of work is important. This kind of work is beautiful. Ultimately, I hope you find in these pages an invitation—God is at work in Canada, so it's time to step out and try something new. It might be time to try something gutsy yourself!

Acknowledgements

There are so many people that contributed to this book in one way or another. First I would like to thank all of the pioneer planters that participated in the study. Thank you for your bravery and honesty in sharing your journey with me. I hope I have honoured your stories. Thank-you to Joe Manafo for the many late night conversations and for inspiring this book with your documentary. Thank-you to David Fitch, Dan Sheffield, and James Watson for your helpful comments and encouragements in the early days of my research and writing. Thank-you to Jay Dyrland and Leighton Tebay for the coffee chats as I was formulating my ideas. Thanks to the New Leaf Network for your unending inspiration. You give me hope for our future. Thank-you St. Bosco Edits for your invaluable work. Thank-you to my sons for staying patient and quiet while we shared office space. Thank-you to my wife Katherine for believing this book could and should be written.

Made in the USA
San Bernardino, CA
15 November 2016